MW00906226

Emotions Simplified

Feel the Way You Want When You Want

Emina Karamanovski, MD

iUniverse, Inc.
New York Lincoln Shanghai

Emotions Simplified
Feel the Way You Want When You Want

Copyright © 2008 by Emina Karamanovski

All rights reserved. No part of this book may be used or reproduced by any means, graphic, electronic, or mechanical, including photocopying, recording, taping or by any information storage retrieval system without the written permission of the publisher except in the case of brief quotations embodied in critical articles and reviews.

iUniverse books may be ordered through booksellers or by contacting:

iUniverse
2021 Pine Lake Road, Suite 100
Lincoln, NE 68512
www.iuniverse.com
1-800-Authors (1-800-288-4677)

Because of the dynamic nature of the Internet, any Web addresses or links contained in this book may have changed since publication and may no longer be valid.

The information, ideas, and suggestions in this book are not intended as a substitute for professional medical advice. Before following any suggestions contained in this book, you should consult your personal physician. Neither the author nor the publisher shall be liable or responsible for any loss or damage allegedly arising as a consequence of your use or application of any information or suggestions in this book.

ISBN: 978-0-595-41731-5 (pbk)
ISBN: 978-0-595-67931-7 (cloth)
ISBN: 978-0-595-86071-5 (ebk)

Printed in the United States of America

Contents

Acknowledgments

I would like to thank my dearest friend and mentor, Joann Calderone, who shared her love for language with me, taught me the subtle meanings of words, and who is still tirelessly helping me improve my English.

Note to the Reader

The purpose of this book is to help you demystify and "domesticate" your emotions. To simplify this complex subject, I will use the terms *emotions* and *feelings* interchangeably.

Introduction

As a native Serbian, I found learning English to be an interesting challenge. I had no idea, however, that mastering the nuances of the English language would lead to an in-depth study of emotions and eventually inspire this book. It all started when I learned the English expression "to push one's buttons." Why do other people know how to push our emotional buttons when we ourselves don't even know what they are? And if other people can push our buttons, shouldn't we be able to push them too?

This curiosity about emotional buttons focused my attention on emotions. This same curiosity started me on a journey of discovering different approaches in positive thinking and holistic healing. How confused and uneducated most of us are about emotions! How often do we hear that we must control our emotions? But it is our ignorance about emotions that needs to be controlled, not the emotions themselves. Emotions are just a form of communication, like words. Would you try to control a language you do not understand?

Society teaches us to value the intellect and downplay our feelings. Yet everything we do is measured on a "feelings" scale; we organize our lives, educate our minds, and train our bodies so that we can *feel* a certain way. We buy a specific house, drive a specific car, obtain a specific degree, do a specific exercise, or wear specific clothes, hoping to achieve a specific feeling, but often fall short of our expectations. We blindly seek to feel a certain way but only occasionally stumble on the desired feeling. Uneducated about our emotions we feel misled and manipulated by our own sentiment and consequently try to control or ignore our feelings, only to end up suffering emotionally as a society. In the last decade, our society has witnessed an increasing number of individuals suffering emotional distress, such as depression, aggression, and panic attacks.

My research on emotions both frustrated and bewildered me. The functioning of the emotional brain and the importance of emotions and emotional intelligence were clearly explained in various publications, however, the purpose and intent of emotions remained unclear; the path to greater emotional intelligence uncharted. Realizing the importance of emotional intelligence gave me permission to acknowledge my feelings and inspired me to seek this new brainpower. But it did not teach me how to become emotionally smarter.

Motivated and determined to understand the purpose of emotions, I became my own experiment. I spent years studying human behavior while examining my thoughts and feelings and resolving my own emotional issues. Along my path of self-exploration, I became a life coach. Focused on emotional matters, my coaching practice catered to individuals troubled by their feelings and seeking emotional clarity, but who had not found solace in conventional therapies.

I understood my clients well. Years ago, I was one of them. After finishing medical school in Belgrade and moving to Canada, away from family and friends and lost in a new culture, I was emotionally hurting. Finding only short-lived relief through counseling, I decided to approach my emotional troubles differently. I studied unconventional approaches that offered the means to emotional well-being, obtained certifications in neurolinguistic programming (NLP) and HeartMath solutions, earned a diploma in logotherapy, and completed a Coach-Ville intensive training before opening my coaching practice in 2000.

Not everyone may be familiar with the coaching profession. Coaching is not therapy but a partnership in which the coach guides the client through a thought-provoking and creative process of self-improvement in order to maximize his or her personal and professional potential.

Analyzing my thoughts and feelings revealed their amazing interconnectedness. Most importantly, it gave me the personal experiences necessary to build a foundation for understanding. As I applied my personal experiences to my coaching practice, the positive transformations demonstrated by my clients corroborated my understanding of emotions and gave birth to this book. No longer just speculation, my theories were tested and validated by human experience.

The purpose of this book is to provide a comprehensive guide to understanding emotions, their various roles, and their significance in enhancing our lives. The true value of emotions is not in how pleasant they are to experience, but in the purpose they intend to serve. Like messengers, emotions inform us about the ways we physically, mentally, and socially engage in various situations. By deciphering their messages, we gain the knowledge and opportunity to make life-changing choices.

The idea of looking for the meaning and purpose of emotions came to me after reading Viktor Frankl's book *Man's Search for Meaning* and studying his philosophy, known as logotherapy. A spirit-centered therapy, logotherapy considers the human spirit, and thus one's character and attitude, as a source of individual strength and health. Comparing his personal experience of surviving Nazi concentration camps to the experiences of others at the camps, Frankl demonstrates that, when confronted with the same extreme circumstances, some individuals experience suffering and desperation, while others feel hope and victory, depending on their personal outlook. His point of view helped me to understand the power of one's attitude as well as the human capacity to deliberately choose that attitude. Since attitude is not a reflection of thoughts, but of feelings, I realized that to choose our attitude we have to pay attention to our feelings. Instead of looking at emotions as whimsical intruders into our lives, I began to see them as meaningful messengers.

In his writing, Frankl suggests that life has meaning under all circumstances, even suffering. Until I was exposed to his point of view, I felt like a victim of a painful, difficult childhood. My father left when I was ten, my mother died when I was fourteen, and I grew up with my sisters in a lower middle-class neighborhood in Belgrade (in the former Yugoslavia, today's Serbia). The explanation I gave for all of my challenging experiences was that life was unfair to me, punishing me undeservedly. Searching for an alternative significance, and guided by Frankl's teaching, I decided to view myself as specially chosen to face my childhood trials, instead of as an unfortunate victim of them. Just as steel is tempered by scorching fire, I chose to believe that the challenges I faced were purposefully designed to develop my skills, strengths, and character.

To my surprise, this new point of view triggered an emotional transformation! The old feeling of being the victim was quickly replaced by that of being a powerful and resourceful person. With new meaning assigned to my life, I found a different way to view my childhood experiences and now realize that my challenges have actually fostered my independence and creativity.

This book is divided into five sections. The first section, "The Anatomy of Emotions," explains the nuts and bolts of emotions and how changing the parts can remodel our emotional experiences. The second section, "Emotional Muscles," describes how emotions, like muscles, have unique roles and thus the ability to "move" us in various directions. For example, we may be paralyzed by fear, distracted by anger, energized by confidence, or propelled by passion. Understanding the different energies associated with our emotions allows us to use feelings to empower our lives.

The third section, "Inner Control Panel" demonstrates our capability to operate our inner energy. Just as control panels have power buttons and dials, we can make decisions that power up our desires and thoughts; we can manipulate the intrinsic expression dial to turn down or light up our personalities. Knowing how to operate our inner control panel puts us in charge of our feelings.

The fourth section is named "Emotion Makeover" because it focuses on the transformational application of emotional intelligence. This section includes emotional fitness exercises designed to help you develop your inner strength and the ability to balance between thinking and feeling, between mind and heart. To feel differently, you have to think differently! The exercises for emotional empowerment are organized around the past, the present, and the future. You will learn to deal with your emotions in retrospect (Cleaning Your Emotional Closet), in the moment (Stress Surfing), and as stones paving the way to your future (Emotion Shopping).

Finally, the last section, "Personal Stories," contains examples of how several emotionally challenging situations have been resolved by using the techniques outlined here. The transformational examples are presented as a tool to help you to review the practical application of the shared information. Besides my personal experiences that are shared throughout the book, you will read numerous examples of my clients who experienced emotional transformation. Their names have been changed and stories slightly modified to protect their privacy.

This book is geared toward everyday life; it is not about trying to justify why you feel a certain way, but rather understanding and transforming the present. The ideas offered are for you to apply any time, in any situation. You may be an executive having a difficulty controlling your temper, a manager frustrated with an employee, a parent overwhelmed with duties, or a person disappointed and flustered with life not turning the way you expected; nevertheless, the emotional challenges you face are common to every human being. For that reason, this book is written to *you*.

Whether you choose to read only the personal stories section or you venture into more in-depth study of emotions, my intention is to challenge your old ways of thinking. I hope that the material provided in this book will shine a different light on emotions and help you put your hands on and arms around your feelings. With greater understanding, what once seemed like a wilderness of unknown dangers can become a treasure map to better life experiences. Yes, you *can* push your own emotional buttons!

PART ONE
The Anatomy of Emotions

It takes a lot of courage to release the familiar and seemingly secure, to embrace the new. But there is no real security in what is no longer meaningful. There is more security in the adventurous and exciting, for in movement there is life, and in change there is power.

Alan Cohen

Fascinated with understanding and managing emotions, I became both the patient and the doctor for my emotional problems. Identifying and treating troublesome feelings became my passionate obsession, which led me to discover that, yes, we can choose our emotions. Not only do we have the power to decide how we want to feel about our lives, we also have the authority to execute these decisions.

We are the sole proprietors of our feelings; nobody can feel our feelings. Others can empathize with us, recognize that our emotional experience resonates with their own; nevertheless, our feelings belong to us. The same is true for our capacity to make decisions: Someone can suggest or impose a choice upon us, but nobody can decide for us the attitude we take toward a forced choice. We can decide to be indifferent or defiant and stand our position against authority.

Although it is a widely used word, the meaning of emotion is not easy to explain or understand. According to the *American Heritage* dictionary, the definitions of emotion are 1) a mental state that arises spontaneously rather than through conscious effort and 2) a state of mental agitation or disturbance. At the times when our emotional buttons are pushed we are surprised and often overwhelmed by our feelings. Our bodies infused with sensations and our minds flooded with racing thoughts, emotions take over our lives like sudden intruders. Showing up with no apparent rhyme or reason, emotions are consequently viewed as forces that need to be controlled instead of examined and learned from.

"The Anatomy of Emotions" explains the purpose and structure of feelings so that you can understand that emotions are not intruders needing your disciplinary intervention, but rather organized and purposeful heralds calling you to action. Rather than seeing them as the enemy, you can recognize emotions as friendly messengers providing you with valuable information. As thoughts help you interpret the world emotions provide you with information about your involvement in the world; thoughts tell you *what* and emotions tell you *how*. By learning the nuts and bolts that comprise your emotional anatomy, you can learn how to rebuild and redesign your emotional experiences—and thereby choose how you want to engage in life.

Chapter One
What Are Emotions?

Emotions are often stigmatized in the same manner as is the IRS. Because of their overpowering nature, people view emotions as annoying intruders. Their intentions are often misunderstood, and their messages ignored or neglected. We would be better served to accept them with an open mind, as emotions are messengers informing us about the unique ways we are involved in various circumstances. Our feelings uncover specifics about our engagement in life: passion indicates that we are absorbed, apathy that we are disengaged, and hatred that we are strongly opposed. When emotions enter our awareness, they alert us to something in need of our attention. By understanding the messages of emotions and considering the information that they provide, we can turn any situation into an opportunity to decide deliberately how we want to engage in life.

Imagine receiving a letter from the IRS in your mail. You glimpse at the ominous red print IMPORTANT on the envelope. Suddenly, you're petrified. Heart pounding, mouth drier by the second, you gingerly drop the now threatening envelope on your mail pile and try to ignore it. But your imagination goes wild. Obsessively, you agonize: What did I do wrong? How much do I have to pay? Where will I ever find the money?

After some period of self-torture, you finally gather enough courage to open the letter—only to find that the IRS is just updating their system and needs you to confirm your personal information. Emotionally drained and limp with relief, you fill out the provided form and mail the envelope with a sense of liberation. Everything is in order again.

Different outcomes could have occurred in the scenario I've just described, but regardless of the result, you are in the dark until you open the envelope. All of the worry and confusion was created by your lack of knowledge, not by the content of the letter. You don't know where you stand in any situation, nor do you know your options or possible responses, until you comprehend the circumstances and your relationship to those circumstances. Feelings are sensors and gauges providing you with information so that you can relate to life physically, mentally, and socially.

Imagine sensing a change of temperature in your environment. You interpret the feeling as being cold, evaluate the degree of your discomfort, and then you decide whether to take action. You judge possible solutions, such as turning on the heat or getting a sweater. You may decide to take action, rationalize that the discomfort is temporary, or accept that you are too lazy to do anything about it. You may get sick the next day and remember that you ignored the chilled feeling. Nevertheless, what is important is that you received the message and learned from it.

In his book *Emotional Intelligence*, author Daniel Goleman explains, "The fact that the thinking brain grew from the emotional reveals much about the relationship of thought to feeling; there was an emotional brain long before there was a rational one." In our personal evolution, first we feel, then we learn the words to describe our feelings. We experience and store most of our emotional memories long before we learn the words to verbalize our feelings and before we have the ability to comprehend their meaning. For the same reason, most people have felt something they cannot easily explain.

We grow up mentally educated but emotionally illiterate. We know the words for emotions but are generally incapable of identifying the feelings that match them. Lacking a full emotional vocabulary, we simplify the way we describe our feelings by merely categorizing them as good or bad, up or down, unaware that by doing so we deprive ourselves of valuable tools for comprehension, interaction, and expression. Like early cavemen, in this area we simply haven't evolved.

Imagine if we were incapable of tasting any flavors but sweet and bitter. What a boring life that would be! Like spices, feelings give flavor to our experiences. The more receptive we are to our feelings, the better we can savor the unique flavors of our lives. The better we become at distinguishing subtle differences in our feelings, the more flavorful life's experiences become. The more bravely and directly we are willing to receive the messages our emotions bring, the better understanding we have of the possible options and the greater personal ability we have to control the overall outcome. Learning to identify various emotions and feelings is like tasting an exotic dish or a glass of wine: it takes willingness, curiosity and practice.

Victims of their emotional illiteracy, people often feel confused, overwhelmed, or stalled by their emotions. Take for example Paul, a twenty-two-year-old recent college graduate and aspiring writer. When Paul finished college and returned home to Dallas to look for a job, his mother suggested that he pay me a visit. Paul felt depressed and discouraged. Looking at Paul's dull facial expression and slow movements, I wondered what was bothering him. Here was a young, bright, healthy man with endless possibilities to explore life, and he was spending his time alone, crying.

Paul explained, "I feel judged because of my depression. I feel worse since I came back home because while I was in school, classes provided distraction. I also like to journal, but I keep writing the same thing repeatedly. I lack creativity to write, and I cannot shed the feeling of depression. I feel stuck."

From an emotional standpoint, depression, like stress, is a *state* representing an amalgam of feelings. Depending on their combined intention, the sum of various feelings can cause a state of depression or stress. For example, fear and hopelessness can cause a person's state of energy to be low and down-turned (i.e., "depressed") while anxiety and frustration can create internal strain (i.e., a stressful state). It is by identifying and transforming the contributing feelings that the state can change. In order for Paul to feel differently, he needed to discover and identify the underlying feelings causing his depressed state.

"I feel sadness," Paul said. "Sadness is different than being sad; when you are sad, you have a reason to feel sad, but in sadness, it is like nothing is happening, and you are stagnant." Because his description of sadness indicated boredom, I decided to further my questioning. In a second attempt to clarify his emotional state, Paul was to come up with five other words, other than depression and sadness, to describe his feelings. He identified the following feelings: pressured, hopeless, purposeless, overwhelmed, and alienated. Once his feelings were identified, Paul and I were able to address them individually and explore their messages.

Feeling pressured was Paul's first emotion. As an aspiring professional writer, Paul felt compelled to "produce" a book rapidly, start making money, move out of his parents' house, and pay off his student loans. Paul had unrealistic expectations that were setting him up to fail.

His second identified feeling was hopelessness. As he explained, Paul kept writing the same thing repeatedly. Although this phenomenon is common among writers, Paul had difficulty accepting it as a normal phase in the business of writing. Instead of waiting for the writer's block to pass and for a wave of creativity to come, Paul began doubting his ability as a writer.

Continuing to examine his emotions, the feeling of purposeless uncovered another aspect of the same writer's block problem: "I am given a gift but wasting it and causing disappointment to my parents and everyone who believed in me."

The skill that he had spent years honing in college and had hoped would give purpose to his life seemed to be beyond his reach.

Furthermore, being overwhelmed encompassed all previously mentioned feelings. He felt pressured to write so he could make a living and pay off his debts, but pressure suffocated his creativity and exacerbated his writer's block, which in turn produced doubt and feelings of purposeless and hopeless. By changing his expectations about the "book production," he took the weight off his shoulders.

There was one more feeling left to be examined: the feeling of alienation. When describing the meaning of alienation, Paul explained that his inspiration for writing usually came from the intimate relationships with his friends or his partner. Writing required him to spend long hours alone, but away from friends and single, Paul felt "people deprived" and thus separated from his inspiration. Separation from others was an additional cause of his depressed state.

Emotions are messengers helping us to understand our situation; the more specific we are in understanding their messages, the easier it is to find solutions to our situation. The solution to Paul's situation was finding a social activity or profession that would connect him with people of his age or who shared his interests. We explored other employment options, and for the first time, Paul considered teaching. The solution became apparent, and Paul's emotional state changed. With the emotional dent repaired, Paul felt motivated and confident again.

Identifying emotions does not happen spontaneously. It requires mindfulness and an attention to detail. As a foreigner concerned with clarity of communication and understanding, my attention to words and their context is heightened in comparison to native English speakers. Because I must consciously learn, rather than unconsciously absorb English expressions, I often miss their "common" meanings but notice meanings hidden to others.

I discovered that many people use the phrase "You know what I mean?" to cover up emotional illiteracy. How often have you found yourself saying this when you are struggling to express feelings or ideas that are not clear to you? After you've heard someone use this expression, have you ever wondered if you really knew what the other person meant and whether the two of you were thinking similarly in that specific situation?

Probably not. Like most people, you acquiesced and assumed that you understood the implied meaning. After all, you didn't want to interrogate the other person. You wanted to be polite and avoid hurting her feelings or making her uncomfortable.

When we assume the other person's meaning, we inevitably imagine more or less, but seldom exactly what she means. Consequently, miscommunication happens … constantly.

It is natural that we struggle with emotional matters. We are emotionally involved in life but unprepared to deal with our feelings. Instead of being discouraged or annoyed by our incapacity to understand our feelings, we have to learn to welcome and give voice to our emotions. Recognizing their helpful intention and heeding their messages provides us with valuable information so that we can govern our lives.

Similar to a mail carrier delivering mail to a specific destination, emotions deliver messages personally addressed to you. You are the sole proprietor of your feelings, and it is your responsibility to receive and open your "emotion-mail." Read it, consider your options, and choose your response.

Chapter Two
What is the Purpose of Emotions?

The purpose of emotions has long been a mystery. Consequently, emotions have been devalued and the value of the intellect inflated. Society reminds us repeatedly that to succeed in business you have to "check your emotions at the door." In business—and in the world in general—showing sentiment puts you at risk of being labeled "emotional" and, thus, summarily rejected. With such bad publicity, feelings became undesired, something to be controlled, repressed, or better yet, avoided.

Undeniably, emotions can at times be rowdy trespassers, affecting our capacity to think and make sound judgments. But when only aware of their disruptive behavior, we mistakenly view emotions and thoughts as rivals. Antonio Damasio, an internationally recognized neurologist, explains in his book *Descartes' Error* that reason may not be as pure as most of us think, and that emotions and feelings may not be intruders of reason, but actually enmeshed in the intellect.

However, feeling and thinking are equally important human functions. If we consider one function more valuable than the other, we will be unbalanced. Intellectual activities, whether memorizing or reasoning, actually depend on our capacity to feel. In studying the development of the human brain, we learn that the emotional areas develop before the cognitive areas and even assist our neocortex—the part of the brain considered to be the seat of thought—in its functioning. The first part of the brain to develop regulates basic functioning, such as breathing and digesting; the second part to develop processes sensory information; and the third comprehends what the senses perceive. As humans evolved, our sense of smell helped us learn and remember which foods were safe to consume. Distinguishing among smells, recognizing them, comparing a present smell with past ones, and discriminating good food from bad food preceded reasoning and logical thinking.

As the center of "higher" brain function, the neocortex brings together thoughts and feelings; it enhances an emotion by adding what we think about it and improves our thinking by allowing us to have feelings about ideas or images.

What we think of as logical is usually felt a certain way internally. Read the following words while paying attention to how they feel: "clear and loud," and "loud and clear." Although the words used are the same, their meanings feel different to you. Depending on the sequence of the words, one combination feels "right" and, hence, logical, while the other does not. Can you now comprehend how logic depends on feeling the correct sequence of words or thoughts? We memorize a specific sequence and consider it "logical." Interestingly, when people seem to derail from a conventional train of thought, we label them as "unreasonable," but when we want people to be creative, we encourage them to think "outside of the box." Does this mean that creative thinking is illogical or unreasonable?

Every organ in the body has a specific function. It is not a fluke that feelings are associated with skin. Skin is the largest human organ, and its most obvious function is to provide a protective barrier for our body. Like skin, our feelings form a boundary between us and our environment, but it is an emotional boundary rather than a physical one. A less obvious but perhaps more intriguing function of the skin is to assist us in our survival. Leprosy patients cannot feel their skin, and because they cannot therefore sense danger, they can burn themselves or bleed to death. Similarly, if we numb our sentiment and ignore our capacity to feel, we can risk extinguishing our emotional lives.

Emotions serve the definitive purpose of assisting us in self-discovery, self-expression, and self-actualization. The foremost purpose of feeling is to help us discover and demonstrate our uniqueness. Imagine being emotionless. How would you or anyone else know who you are? Stripped of feelings, you would become a robot with no personality.

There are six billion people on the planet, yet each of us is individually unique. We are born with a predisposition for, but not an awareness of, our uniqueness and splendor. We are born like rose buds and given a lifetime to bloom. Emotions assist us in our personal development; they help us discover who we are, what we like or dislike, and what we stand for. Feelings help us recognize our affinities and reveal our idiosyncrasies. They assist us in expressing our personalities and conveying our values. Feelings allow us to demonstrate our attitudes and reach our personal potential, as in being brave, speaking one's truth, or transforming one's predicament into achievement.

Someone once said that to know yourself you have to sit still, wait, and meditate, but to *be* yourself you have to act. In other words, to learn who you are, you have to feel yourself, but to express who you are, you have to put yourself out there for others to feel you.

Looking at the human genome, our uniqueness is less obvious, but observing human personality, our individuality becomes more apparent. The definition of the word *unique* misleads us to identify individuality as something unusual, as one specific trait that sets us apart from one another. Actually, our individuality represents a unique *combination* of common human characteristics. For instance, many people are thoughtful, but the level of attentiveness and expression differentiates one individual from another. The subtle differences we sense in the realm of feelings provide us with nuances of personal characteristics needed to demonstrate our authenticity. For example, two people can express an affinity for a specific subject or task, however, they can differ in the degree of their affinity; one person may feel "like" while the other person can feel "passion" for the subject or task in question.

A friend of mine majored in history and studied art while preparing for medical school. To others, his choice was not "logical" because it did not reflect the popular sequence of school courses. However, while following his passion, he also sharpened his writing skills and refined his aesthetic eye. During his specialization in plastic surgery, passion and practicality came together for him. Not only did he pioneer several important advances in medicine, he had the ability to write about them as well. By age thirty-six, he became the most literarily prolific plastic surgeon in the United States for his age group, with three major textbooks and thousands of articles written. He stood out among other physicians because of the extraordinary expression of his passion. Self-expression is our ability to use feelings to demonstrate our individuality.

Beyond assisting us in self-discovery and self-expression, feelings contribute in the process of self-actualization by helping us to materialize our ideas, desires, and potentials. Self-actualization is our capacity to transcend the intellectual and spiritual status-quo and expand beyond the limitations of our personalities. For example, feelings of courage, determination, and faith help us rise above or go beyond fear, insecurity, and doubt. The author Sam Keen, in his book *Learning to Fly,* explains our need for self-actualization: "Humankind cannot live by bread and business alone. We have an instinctual need for self-transcendence and ecstasy."

Our feelings are messengers, but we decide their purpose, i.e., whether we will allow them to serve in our journey of self-discovery, self-expression, or self-actualization. Imagine that someone angers you by making a condescending comment about your business idea. Anger is the messenger telling you that someone has violated your values. To determine the purpose of its message, you have three options. First, you can discover that the reason for your anger was the disrespect shown toward your idea. In this situation, anger made you realize that supporting people in accomplishing their dreams is something that you—not the other person—value. Second, you can evaluate that it is important to express what matters to you and inform the other person about it. Finally, you can interpret anger as an opportunity to readjust your attitude toward your own dream. Instead of being upset by other people's disapproval, you can choose to be confident and decisive about actualizing your business idea.

All three processes—self-discovery, expression, and actualization—are happening simultaneously. Throughout life, while we keep rediscovering ourselves, we continue adding more facets to our personalities. Our likes and dislikes change, our awareness of the world matures, and our priorities evolve, while our feelings keep us continually informed about these changes. As we gather experiences, our feelings store them as colorful memories. Without feelings our lives would be dull and our earthly presence unmemorable.

Chapter Three
Solving the Emotional Puzzle

In the same way that it takes two to tango, it takes *you* (your unique personality traits and beliefs) and a *situation* in order for emotions to occur. Experiencing emotions indicates that you are involved in some situation; otherwise, you would be indifferent. If there is nothing happening around you, you feel nothing. And if there are a lot of things happening but you are not interested in them, you still feel zilch. The way you engage in a given situation may not always be obvious; it could be conscious or unconscious, but the existence of any feeling confirms your involvement.

Emotions don't just happen. There has to be a specific set of circumstances in place for a specific emotion to arise. For example, jealousy arises in a situation where one person's social position seems endangered. Let's say Julie and her boyfriend Peter are at a party. Peter is having an animated conversation with Suzie, who appears to be equally enthralled. Julie feels jealousy toward Suzie. In order for Julie to feel jealous she has to perceive a possibility of Suzie taking her partner, otherwise she would not be jealous. Julie has to believe that Suzie has something appealing to Peter, such as a better-looking body. If Suzie is a much older lady, Julie may not sense any threat and thus would not be jealous. If Julie feels quite secure in her relationship, she may interpret the situation as nothing more than a friendly conversation.

Our emotional experiences are built from two structural components: one, the combination of the circumstances in which we find ourselves and, two, our personal interpretation of those circumstances. Thus, emotions work like puzzles: each feeling is a unique combination of the structural parts, i.e., our circumstances and our interpretation of those circumstances. If the circumstances were different—say, Julie and Suzie conversing without Peter—Julie might have felt envious of Suzie's figure, but she would not be jealous. If the perception were different—if Julie did not perceive Suzie as the competition—there would be no interpretation of threat and consequently, no jealousy.

People participate in events by noticing a part of what is happening. Perception is not what we see but what we pay attention to in a given situation. Each emotion describes a specific set of circumstances with a mixture of subtleties and intricacies. What we perceive as interesting or important directly affects our feelings. When I came to Canada, I noticed only things that were different from my usual surroundings: streets were larger, cars were bigger, winter was colder, and people were more distant. Consequently, I felt "different," hence rejected and lonely. Then, motivated by my desire to make Canada home, I decided to change my perception. As I focused on what we had in common, people became more approachable and friendlier. My emotions changed to feelings of happiness, acceptance, and appreciation.

We experience emotions mentally through thinking and physically through sensing. There are two distinct elements to every emotion:

- The mental element is what we perceive and how we understand, explain, and relate to the external conditions around. This element is about the meaning of emotions, which could be both impersonal and personal. The impersonal meaning explains the common set of circumstances required for an emotion to occur, while the personal meaning describes the individual significance assigned to an event or experience.

- The physical element is the bodily sensation elicited by an individual feeling, including the awareness of our inner energy associated with emotions. When we describe our feelings as up or down, intense or mild, we are actually commenting on the state of our inner energy. Different philosophies refer to this energy as life force, chi, ki, or prana; we all experience it but are frequently unaware of its presence. Recognition of this vital force leads to understanding how feelings and emotions, which are essentially the same, reflect the state of our inner energy. In the second part of the book, Emotional Muscles, you will learn more about the physical sensations associated with feelings.

Once we understand both the mental and physical elements of feelings we are able to live with greater awareness and choice. Dictionary definitions often supply synonyms—words for similar emotions—but fail to describe the circumstances in which they appear. For example, the *Webster Universal College* dictionary describes admiration as a feeling of pleasure, wonder, and approval, and anger as a strong feeling of displeasure or hostility. Descriptions such as these merely qualify a feeling rather than explain it.

To comprehend the messages of emotions we have to look at the context in which they occur. For example, admiration describes feelings of approval, respect, and wonder experienced about another person's character or behavior, whereas anger depicts a situation in which someone's attitude or behavior violates another person's important personal principles.

Although some feelings overlap, the details of their components make them distinctive. Consider the differences between the feelings of determination and stubbornness. Although these two feelings may occur in the same situation, their messages communicate quite different meanings. According to the *American Heritage and Webster Universal College* dictionaries, the definition of stubborn is "unreasonably unyielding, firmly resolved, or determined." The same dictionary's definition of determined is "marked by determination," and determination is explained as "the act of making and arriving at a decision," as well as "firmness of purpose."

The key difference between these two feelings is focus. While a stubborn person is unreasonably unyielding, a determined person is purposely centered. We generally characterize determination as positive and stubbornness as negative. When a person's goal is to *resist* something or someone, he's considered stubborn, while a determined person is focused on *attaining* a goal. Rather than wasting energy on stubborn resistance, the emotionally aware individual chooses to transform stubbornness into determination. That emotional shift alone will free up the energy needed to propel him toward his desired goal.

The way we interpret a situation and the meaning we assign to an event combine to form our emotional experience. The *American Heritage* dictionary definition of meaning is "intrinsic value," but also "implication" and "application." Following this explanation, the concept of meaning appears to have two dimensions: the inherent value embedded in the things themselves, and the value found outside of things, in the perception of their usefulness or significance. A one-dollar bill always has the same inherent value of one hundred cents, but its relative value changes according to our needs.

The meaning and the personal value assigned to a one-dollar bill is completely individual. Likewise, it is not the intrinsic value of things and events, but the personal meaning we assign to them, that matters. When something is meaningful to you, it means that a person or an event holds significance. What we consciously or unconsciously recognize as important resonates within us as emotion. If nothing is important or meaningful, then we are indifferent and have no emotional experiences at all! In his book *Meditations,* the great Roman emperor and philosopher, Marcus Aurelius, observed that, "If you are distressed by anything external, the pain is not due to the thing itself, but to your estimate of it; and this you have the power to revoke at any moment."

I was the youngest of five. If I broke a glass or came home five minutes late, my mother would slap the palms of my extended hands with a wooden spoon. If I pulled my hands back to avoid the slaps, my mother would add another one. And if I cried, my mother would then confine me to another room to learn how to "behave." I was supposed to stand there taking what I "deserved" like a "grown-up." With experience, I developed a way of holding my elbows tight to my body so that I could proudly take what I "deserved."

My father left when I was ten. My mother died when I was fourteen. As I finished medical school, war started in my native country. I moved to Canada when I was twenty-six. No judgment was attached to these events. Life just went on.

After a few years in Canada, by watching television and reading news, I learned that slapping hands was considered a form of child abuse. All of a sudden, my pride in withstanding my mother's discipline vanished. I became a victim. From that point on, every challenge I encountered was colored with a sense of disadvantage. Interestingly, I started to *feel* like a victim—insecure and powerless. As life challenged me with new experiences, I didn't like the new way I felt about myself. I had once felt confident, courageous, and proud. But that was before I thought of myself as an abused child.

Although I didn't like the way I felt, I couldn't go back to feeling as I did before. My capacity to withstand the pain and take the punishment didn't bring up pride anymore. The unfairness of the situation prevailed. In order to change the way I felt, I had to understand the situation and assign it a new meaning.

From the perspective of a mature person, hand slapping and child abuse looked different. To abuse someone meant to intentionally inflict pain and suffering. What was my mother's intention? Was her intent really to hurt me? Considering the synonyms and antonyms of the verb "to abuse" clarified its meaning; the synonyms were to mistreat, exploit, or neglect, and the antonyms were to protect or compliment. My mother's disciplinary action did not match a synonym of the word *abuse*. She was rather protective of me. Furthermore, to abuse meant that the person being abused was weak and powerless to have an effect on mistreatment. How much did I really "suffer" from it? Did hand slapping take away any of my power? And, what power are we talking about? Is it my power to decide?

Then I remembered another incident. Long ago my girlfriend got a color TV—the first color TV I'd seen. We were playing together, and it was about time for me to go home. But the cartoon was just about to start, and it would be in color! I knew what would happen if I got home late, and yet I was mesmerized by the TV wonder. I stayed five minutes longer than I should have, and then I ran home and took the slaps I deserved.

The magical five minutes of a cartoon in color was worth five hand slaps … Interestingly, the hand slapping that time was not traumatizing. Looking back, I realized that even as a child, I made my own choices. Although I didn't like to have my hands slapped, I chose to watch the cartoon and bear the consequences. The experience of watching the cartoon in color held more meaning for me than the pain of the wooden spoon hitting my palms.

It was surprising to discover that because of that cartoon I was not suffering the consequences of my choice. It seemed like a fair trade—I knew up front the cost of my choice, and I paid for it. According to my memory, I wasn't all that powerless. After all, I *chose* to watch that cartoon! My mother didn't mean to abuse me. She only knew an old European way of discipline. My mother was born in Yugoslavia in 1919. Raised by parents who were born in the previous century, my mother just repeated the parenting lessons she learned from hers. She didn't punish me because she intended to hurt me. Her intent was not to mistreat me, but to teach me to be a responsible and accountable person. I may not choose her way of teaching, but I have chosen to be responsible and accountable. And this was something I could feel proud about again.

In *Man's Search for Meaning,* Viktor Frankl tells us, "For the meaning of life differs from man to man, from day to day, and from hour to hour. What matters, therefore, is not the meaning of life in general but rather the specific meaning of a person's life at a given moment." In the story of my childhood discipline, as the meaning of my experience changed to match my priorities and awareness, my emotions changed accordingly. The *circumstances*—the way my mother disciplined me—remained the same. My *perception* of the circumstances and of myself within those circumstances changed.

At first, hand slapping was a limited choice offered to a child to learn the consequence of not following her mother's rules. Next, it was associated with child abuse: hand slapping was a meaningless act, a source of suffering, with my mother as the tyrant and me as the helpless victim. After recognizing the detrimental effect of viewing my childhood experience as abusive, hand slapping evolved into another meaning. In its third meaning, I became a powerful decision making person and my mother a teacher, and the hand slapping was transformed into lessons about personal values.

Our thinking affects our feelings and vice versa. The way you perceive your qualities and capacities will determine the feelings you have about yourself. If you think you are capable of doing something, you feel confident and resolute. In addition, if someone gives you a compliment and you interpret it as a meaningful evaluation of your skills, you could feel a surge of energy and self-worth. Similarly, the way you perceive your feelings can influence your thinking. If you feel apprehension about a specific meeting because someone suggested it might be a fierce interrogation, you could misinterpret your feelings as a lack of competency, and you could mentally freeze.

To benefit from the messages of your emotions, you have to engage your thinking in a different way. You have to become mindful of your feelings and start asking yourself questions. What is the meaning of this feeling and what would be its opposite? Which feelings are similar, and how are they different? Do these feelings differ in the circumstances that elicit them or in the way you engage in those circumstances? What does the situation mean to you? What action does it inspire you to take?

Consider the feeling of frustration. The message or meaning of frustration is that we are engaged in unsuccessful, fruitless action. What other feeling describes unsuccessful action? One example is disappointment, which can also signify our failure to attain a desired objective. What is the difference between the two words? Both feelings stem from a situation where we desire something but our desire is not met. When frustrated, the desired outcome is still out in front of us; we still have hope for attaining it. When disappointed, what we wish seems gone because we have lost hope for obtaining the desired outcome. By understanding the specific message of each emotion, we can choose the best course of action. In frustration, we can reevaluate the approach or redefine the desired outcome, so our action bears fruit, while in disappointment, we can either reestablish hope or let go of the old expectation and set up a new one. (For more information on the meanings of emotions, please refer to table 3 in the "Tables" section.)

As mentioned earlier, the meaning associated with emotions is a mixture of impersonal and personal interpretation. Considering the intertwined nature of these two interpretations, the most challenging part of understanding our emotions is uncovering the personal meaning that triggers our feelings. Although understanding the impersonal meaning of emotions requires explorative thinking, discovering the personal meaning requires investigation and sophistication. Each individual has layers of intertwined beliefs affecting her feelings. The following example demonstrates how seemingly unrelated beliefs and their associated values could trigger an emotional reaction.

Sherry was a newlywed. She and her husband, Todd, were not a full year out of college, still struggling to find the right jobs. Sherry was upset about something her husband had done, and she felt hostile and extremely angry. In Todd's first year of college, he applied for and obtained a credit card, purchased something, and then moved to a different state, forgetting to pay the bill. Four years later, the bill collector found him. Although penalties were added to the bill, the balance was manageable, yet Sherry was furious about the situation. Todd tried to apologize for the inconvenience, explained that it was a mistake, that it would not affect his credit score, that they had money to pay the bill, and that the situation was not as terrible as she was making it out to be. Still, nothing was calming her down.

Since Sherry was seeing me professionally, we both looked at the situation and concluded that the extent of her anger was not proportional to the gravity of the situation. Sherry still could not let go of her anger. The situation had triggered some important feelings that she could not dismiss. As we explored the meaning of Todd's behavior, Sherry discovered that her assumption was that his negligence indicated irresponsibility. She was angry because Todd had violated her values of personal and financial accountability. We examined Todd's behavior in various situations where he demonstrated a great sense of responsibility and concluded that one incident was not sufficient to override his overall quality. Sherry felt less angry but still unsettled in her feelings. There was something else bothering her. She somehow felt anxious and threatened by the idea of him possibly being irresponsible. Anxiety is a sign that a person is feeling unprepared for something in the future. While examining Sherry's anxiety, we discovered that she was contemplating having a family and feared that going forward would be a mistake if Todd was truly irresponsible. Sherry felt that it would be unwise to bring children into the world if the father was not dependable. She loved Todd and wanted to have a family with him, yet she felt confused and scared. She could not go to Todd for help or advice, as he was her worry. Viewing the situation as relevant to possibly making a major life mistake explains the extent of Sherry's anger.

The meaning Sherry attached to the situation was too serious and seemingly unrelated to the facts themselves, but planning her future family was personally important. By questioning the meaning assigned to Todd's behavior, Sherry was finally able to see the absurdity of her association and worry. Her anger melted; she was free to accept the credit card incident as an accident. She realized how much personal and financial responsibility meant to her and was able to acknowledge that Todd had those qualities. Learning from the experience, Sherry addressed the issue of accountability with her husband, which further improved their communication.

Personal and impersonal meanings overlap, and learning to differentiate between them takes time. Impersonal meaning has the consistency of a definite setting, a specific set of circumstances associated with a specific feeling, while personal meanings are subject to free association and thereby more difficult to decipher. For example, the impersonal meaning of anger is that someone has violated our personal values. Uncovering which value has been violated is about revealing personal meaning. Because of their commonality and consistency, understanding the impersonal meaning of emotions is always a good place to start.

Since there is no simple way to uncover the relationship between emotions and the meaning we have personally assigned to a given situation, let us examine together another example from my coaching practice.

Jim was in his third marriage when he decided he needed professional help. Infidelity had destroyed his previous two marriages. Jim's third wife was special to him; he really loved and cared for her. Jim wanted to stay faithful to his wife but had a difficult time resisting the temptation of other women. He felt confused, disappointed, and angry at his own weakness. He was violating his own values of commitment. Acting as his coach, I helped Jim to explore the meanings associated with his situation.

Jim rationalized his unfaithfulness, saying, "It's genetic; my father did it, my grandfather did it, and my great-grandfather cheated on his wife." Considering the family history of unfaithfulness, Jim attributed his behavior to a seemingly genetic defect—an "unfaithful gene"—that made him long for extramarital relationships and also made him too weak to withstand the attraction. With such an interpretation, it was obvious why Jim felt he could not resist the temptation. From Jim's point of view, his unfaithful gene was the culprit of his strong desires and lack of willpower.

The problem was not Jim's genetics but his perception. To create an emotional change, it was necessary to strengthen Jim's internal power and diminish the external attraction. The first step in accomplishing our goal was to rename the unfaithful gene to a "genetic predisposition." Jim had to understand that, instead of being a victim of his genes, he had a predisposition for a specific condition, but he was in control. His situation was similar to driving a car that pulls to one side: to create an emotional change, the driver has to be aware of the "pulling condition" and not obsess about it but adjust his grip and keep his focus on the road.

Once Jim understood that he had the power to override his desire, we proceeded to explore what triggered his genetic predisposition. We looked for the times when he felt the desire to seek another female companion and discovered that it happened whenever he felt lonely, unnoticed, or unappreciated by his wife. Feeling disconnected from his relationship, Jim felt anxious, sad, and rejected, but mostly not desired. The feeling of being undesired drew his attention to other females and fueled his attraction to them.

Jim's wife may have been distant, but the problem arose when Jim took her distance personally, interpreting her behavior as a lack of interest in him. Examining the times when Jim felt a lack of emotional connection with his wife, he realized that his wife was emotionally unavailable because she was preoccupied with something and not because she wasn't interested in Jim. He speculated that at those same times she probably felt lonely and needed his support as much as he needed hers. Jim's feelings shifted; he felt a renewed attraction to his wife and no interest in other women.

When you understand the structural components of emotions and how their interaction affects your feelings, you will know how to transform and redesign your experiences. For example, a colleague makes a belittling comment concerning a work project. Just minutes before the comment, you felt proud and enthusiastic. Afterward, you feel insecure and unsuccessful.

Considering the unpleasant transformation of your feelings in one direction, you can create a transformation in a different direction. You can change your perception of the intent of your colleague's comment. You can willingly decide to evaluate the importance of your colleague's opinion. You can decide how you want to feel about the project in question. You can decide that your colleague is not an expert on the subject and that his opinion is not a valid measurement of your skills or your accomplishments. You can deliberately choose to feel proud and enthusiastic again. You can choose to consider your colleague's comment, think more about your project, and choose to feel determined to make improvements so that you can feel even prouder of yourself.

One out of an extensive collection of quotations by notable Eleanor Roosevelt, the former first lady, says, "No one can make you feel inferior without your consent." In other words, in order to feel a certain way, you have to give importance to something or someone. Someone may force a choice upon you, but you retain the power to choose the meaning and the emotional value you assign to the imposed choice. Nobody can deprive you of your power to choose your attitude.

Too often, we choose unconsciously to value someone else's opinion or judgment over ours. Heeding the message of emotions helps to understand the ways we interact with various situations and consequently provides us with needed information to exercise our personal freedom and power. It is ultimately our own choice to decide the significance of a person or event. Whether we know it or not, we—not others—hold the power to push our own emotional buttons.

Exercise 1
Shifting Gears

The objective of this exercise is to help you experience your capacity to affect your feelings. By changing your perception and the meaning you assign to a given situation, you should experience an emotional shift.

1. Recall a situation when someone's comment upset you. Identify at least three feelings you had at the time of the incident and write them down. Writing is important because it forces you to separate your feelings. When thinking about an emotionally charged situation, your emotions overlap, but when you are writing about the situation, you have no other choice but to address your emotions one at the time.

    _____

    _____

    _____

    _____

    _____

    _____

    _____

    _____

    _____

2. To test how your perception influences your feelings, change the gender of the person involved in the incident, that is, male to female and vice versa. We unconsciously associate different values with gender, which indirectly affects our perception and thus the way we feel about something or someone. Imagine hearing the same offensive comment coming from the "other gender." Observe what happens to your feelings. You would probably internalize the comment slightly differently according to your perception of gender-specific standards and values. Write down your observations.

    _____

    _____

    _____

    _____

    _____

    _____

_____
_____
_____

3. Transform your emotional experience by altering the meaning you assign to the offensive comment. Imagine the person whose comment offended you ten years younger, then ten years older. Depending on a person's age, we place expectations on their expertise and assign different meaning to their comments. Observe what happens with your feelings when you change the offender's age. Write down your observations.

_____
_____
_____
_____
_____
_____
_____
_____
_____

Chapter Four
Beware of Assumptions

Carol was enjoying her first day off after working three weeks in a row. She left her house with the intention of taking care of a few errands, but most specifically she wanted to spend a day without a rigid schedule. Her first stop was the bank. Carol parked her car at a new location, in a spot that did not have a handicapped sign painted on the ground.

As she walked out of the bank, Carol noticed a shoe store nearby and started to wander in when a slow moving police car caught her attention. Carol turned around and glimpsed a man running out of the bank yelling something to the police officer while jabbing his finger furiously in her direction. Curious, and not realizing what the commotion was about, she approached the two men standing on the street. Then she noticed the police officer looking at her car and writing a ticket.

Carol looked up and noticed for the first time a pole with a tiny sign for handicapped parking. She was surprised she hadn't noticed the sign, and then was concerned about being punished for an unintentional act. Red-faced with anger, the bank clerk triumphantly denounced Carol to the stolid police officer: "You see, missy parked at the handicapped place and was about to go shopping," assuming Carol had bad motives for her actions. Upset by his accusations, oblivious of her crime, and innocent in her intention, Carol tried to explain the simple oversight, hoping to rectify their opinion of her. Then she realized that the police officer was just doing his job, that her car was in the wrong place, and that she had to bear the consequences.

The angry bank clerk seemed to hear nothing that Carol said. Steaming with fury, blood pressure skyrocketing, he looked like he was ready to explode. The truth didn't matter to him. Though self-defeating, he had a preset point of view and wasn't willing to give it up. He was the one who had called the police, believing that he was doing the right thing—administering justice.

While his intention was noble, his actions were rude and unfair. He may have been protecting people in need, making sure that no one misused parking spaces dedicated for the handicapped, but he never gave Carol a chance to demonstrate her innocence. With his rigid perception and assumption of her ill-intended action, he built up anger against "people like Carol" and acted unfairly. In his caring, he was selective. If he had broadened his perception and given Carol the benefit of the doubt, he could have asked her if she had noticed parking in the wrong place and by her answer, discovered her true intention. Carol could have been grateful that he had protected her from getting a parking ticket, and he could have felt empowered for the entire day for really helping someone. Instead, because of his narrow-mindedness, he had chosen to punish her, probably felt satisfied for a short period, then angry for the entire day. And all because of the perception he chose.

Understanding the correlation between our perception and our emotional experiences can help us deliberately choose how we relate to any given situation. By changing our perception, we can transform the energy of emotions from unproductive to productive and change our experience of life from misery to fulfillment. For example, if a person has valuable knowledge to share but is afraid to speak in front of a group of colleagues, changing his beliefs about—and indirectly his perception of—the group can free the person from fear and help him deliver the speech. Looking through a lens distorted by fear, the speaker may see the audience as an overwhelming sea of unfriendly faces. If the speaker calibrates his perception and chooses curiosity to look beyond his own fear, he could view his audience as a warmly supportive group of friendly individuals who accept him and wish him success. Instead of believing that the audience is a threat, waiting to attack the speaker, he can choose to believe that the intention of each audience member is to learn something and connect with the speaker. By changing his perception and beliefs, the speaker can transform discomfort into ease about speaking in public. Deliberately choosing courage, he can recognize and overcome the fear by delivering the speech. Remember, whenever you find yourself experiencing a counterproductive feeling, you can transform it by changing your point of view.

Assumptions are perceptual blinders. When you assume something, you make quick judgments and thereby limit your point of view, which further limits your options. Your world view depends on your experiences, your beliefs, and your state of mind in the specific moment in which you are making an assumption. If you have been betrayed by a colleague, your point of view is tinted with suspicion. Consequently, when a colleague makes an innocent comment about your work, you automatically hear it as criticism and an attack. If you believe that your spouse does not care for you, then, when he comes home and acts distant because something worrisome happened at work, you automatically assume that he's ignoring you. Imagine you're focused on a work project, a problem you need to solve. Your business partner offers a solution, but since you are preoccupied with your own search, you dismiss his suggestion. Later on, your business partner makes a sarcastic comment and you assume that he's rude and inconsiderate.

Assumptions are often the culprits causing miscommunications. To test your assumptions and modify your point of view,

1. Question the *intention* of the person involved in a given situation (like in the example of a colleague who makes a sarcastic comment. Is your colleague's intention to hurt or belittle you?).

2. Wonder if there is any other possible *reason* for someone to act a certain way (like in the example of a worrisome spouse. Do you generalize your belief by using the word always–he always does…. Is there any other possible scenario that can explain your spouse's behavior?).

3. Examine what *motivates* someone's attitude or behavior (as in the example of a business partner who makes a sarcastic comment. What is the purpose of your partner's comment? If the purpose is to provoke you and get your attention, could you recall a time when you did not hear her out?).

Let me emphasize. Our perception determines the way we feel about something or someone, and yes, we are in control of our perception. When we act from assumptions, because our point of view is obstructed, our emotional experiences are often distorted. If you are going to a meeting and anticipate an unfavorable outcome, you assume only one possible scenario. For the same reason, when you have a strong emotional reaction to a specific event, you can default to your usual assumption or choose to be curious and question your point of view. Be creative. Look at the intention and/or motivation of the person involved in a specific situation and think of all possible scenarios. In doing so, you may discover your assumption!

PART TWO
Emotional Muscles

No one is truly literate who cannot read his own heart.

Eric Hoffer

Human potential lies in the capacity to use willpower to make decisions. Ironically, we are powerful beings with the capacity to choose and govern our lives, but often we have little conscious awareness of our power. Similar to muscles, our decisions keep us vitally and socially engaged in life, but we use our capacity to make decisions semi-consciously at best. While thinking and feeling give us the ability to decide, the awareness of these functions represents our strength. Fully comprehending our emotions helps us to integrate thinking and feeling, to develop our emotional muscles, and to thereby attain inner stability.

Our energy is our life force—our attitude, our spirit. Although vital to our existence, like the air, our energy goes unnoticed until it moves. Emotions, like energy in motion, inform us about the state and movement of our inner energy. Understanding the sensation of energy associated with our emotions allows us to engage in life with our full capacity.

Thinking positive thoughts works only if we *feel* positive at the same time. We can mentally decide to go in a certain direction, but until we are emotionally committed to the journey, we will not reach our desired destination. The energy associated with emotions is the invisible generator that fuels our creativity and powers our ideas. Emotions are the muscles that put strength into our desires and zest into our actions. Learn to harness their power.

Chapter Five
Understanding Your Inner Energy

We have learned that emotions reflect our involvement in a given situation, but what are they about? Have you ever questioned what it is that you are sensing when experiencing happiness or sadness, pride or shame? Or what really happens when you feel "moved"? The word *emotion* describes what feelings are about; it depicts our inner energy as being in motion (e-motion). This energy is like the air—vital to our existence, but we are unaware of it until it moves.

For centuries, the heart was associated with feelings. Consequently, we refer to a cruel person as a heartless person, or a generous person as a person with a big heart. Putting one's heart into something describes passion, while being rejected by a loved one can leave you with a broken heart. Only recently, we are finding that the connection between the heart and emotions is not simply poetic but scientific. For the past twenty years, scientists have discovered new information about the heart and demonstrated that the heart is more complex than what we believed. The extensive research of one of the early pioneers in neurocardiology, Dr. J. Andrew Armour, reveals that heart has an intrinsic nervous system that is sufficiently sophisticated to act independently of the cranial brain. Thanks to the complexity of the neural web of approximately 40,000 neurons within it, the heart can learn, remember, and sense, which qualifies it as a functional "heart-brain" in its own right (Armour, J., and Ardell, J., eds. *Neurocardiology.* New York: Oxford University Press, 1994).

Moreover, the findings at the Institute of HeartMath show the human heart to be a reliable indicator of our emotional state. The research performed at the Institute shows that heartfelt emotions, such as love, caring, or gratitude produce a smooth, even heart rhythm, which soothes our minds. Disturbing emotions such as anger or anxiety, on the other hand, generate a jagged heart rhythm that affects our capacity to think (Childre, D., and Martin, H., with Beech, D., *The HeartMath Solutions,* New York: HarperSanFrancisco, 1999). This explains why, when emotionally upset, we cannot think clearly. In addition, the unstoppable heartbeat makes the heart the strongest oscillating organ in our body. According to the principle of physics called entrainment, when two oscillating objects are in proximity, they synchronize, and the strongest oscillator entrains the weaker. This principle explains what makes our energy change in the presence of other people, or what makes a group of women living together synchronize in their menstrual periods. Because of entrainment we can feel energized or drained in the presence of certain people. Knowing the principle of entrainment can help us avoid unconscious alignment with energies we judge to be non beneficial.

Furthermore, the heart with its activity—that is, producing electrical stimuli for muscles to contract and for blood to circulate—generates a strong electromagnetic field that extends out farther than current measuring devices can detect. The heart field is five thousand times stronger than the field produced by the brain and at a ten-foot distance can still be detected. In his book, *The Secret Teachings of Plants*, Stephen Harrod Buhner relates, "Between 60 and 65 percent of cells in the heart are neural cells. They are the same kind as those in the brain … [The heart] is a specialized brain that processes specific types of information." The information that the heart processes refers to the characteristics of the electromagnetic field, that is, its presence, strength, and the wave movement within. Since the human heart is born into the proximity of another heart and thus another electromagnetic field, it is sensitive to field vibrations and variations. Heart-to-heart, field-to-field communication is the heart's native tongue. In your lifetime, you have probably had the uncomfortable experience of walking into a room and sensing "thick air," only to later learn that the people in the room had had an argument. At the time, your heart was registering and informing you about the field changes, but you didn't know its language yet.

Whenever the heart experiences an alteration in its electromagnetic spectrum, we, as humans, experience this change as emotions. Throughout life, the heart actively perceives and scans fields, assessing their state and noticing changes in their wave patterns. When we engage in a specific life circumstance that triggers our feelings, the state of our inner energy changes, and our heart-brain alerts us of these changes via our emotions. Consequently, feelings serve as the dashboard of our inner energy. Feelings are sensors and gauges informing us about the patterns and the states of our energy field.

Like the skin can sense a drop in room temperature and inform the body which responds with shivers, the heart can sense anxiety in the environment, send the information to the mind via feelings, and cause the individual to respond with a mood change, such as shifting into alertness or calmness.

When we differentiate feelings as positive and negative, we are seemingly critiquing their purpose, when in reality we are describing the state of our energy. The electromagnetic field generated around the human body creates a wave pattern. The tendency of any wave in ideal conditions (such as a vacuum) is to oscillate in a steady, even pattern and propagate indefinitely. As such, the distinction between "positive" or "negative" feelings describes whether our energy wave patterns are with or against the natural tendency to circulate in a steady manner. The feelings of confidence, appreciation, honesty, or trust are labeled as positive because they describe wave patterns that are steady and free to flow. Conversely, the feelings of insecurity, hatred, or fear are considered negative because they define a state of energy that is irregular and restricted.

The natural behavior of our inner energy is demonstrated in the development of a human being as our tendency to grow and expand. A child is born with limited awareness and capacity to process information, but unrestricted potential. Driven by our innate propensity for personal growth, we learn to think and socially behave while expanding our awareness of self and the world around us. Since our feelings are sensors and gauges informing us about our inner energy, we should stop judging our sentiment and instead recognize that the only useful purpose of defining feelings as positive and negative is to *evaluate* whether our thinking or attitudes promote or restrict our personal development.

To understand our energy it is important to mention that our power to control our energy is our will, which lies uniquely within ourselves. Individually, we have the power to manage our own energy pattern; our will can shape our attitude. We can detect a state or a change in our energy field, such as sensing internal calmness or agitation. We can generate or modify our own energy pattern, such as deciding to be in a good mood. Last but not least, we can affect another person's energy field, but ultimately, we cannot control or be responsible for energy fields other than our own. Although we may trigger a wave of change in someone else, (i.e., we can inspire or push someone's emotional button), we cannot manage what happens afterward. We are responsible for our own energy, and consequently, others are responsible for theirs. No matter how much influence we exert on someone, that individual can always decide what happens with the emotion-wave within his own field. We can accept, reject, ignore, and amplify our feelings, just as we can embrace, refuse, neglect, or intensify one's love. Remember, no one can make you feel anything without your consent.

I occasionally hear people talk about energy vampires—individuals who can hook into your field and "steal" your energy. This is one of many misconceptions about our energy and our feelings. The truth is, our energy field expands beyond our physical body, and when we interact with people our energy fields are touching and interacting. Therefore, yes, others can create disturbance in our energy field, but they can never "steal" or control our energy. Think of a time you fell in love. Daydreaming about your partner, feeling love toward everything and everybody, you were emotionally immune; no energy vampire could burst your "love bubble" and steal your energy.

It is important to reiterate that you are in charge of your energy field. It is in your power to recognize when someone's action or attitude, including your own, is distracting or disturbing your field. When you notice that your energy reserve is low, or that your energy pattern is off balance or scattered, it is your responsibility to take care of yourself. For example, you may feel drained in the presence of a specific person. That person could be one who complains insatiably, while you constantly try to make her happy. You may claim that she is sucking your energy when, in reality, you are wasting your inner energy by misdirecting it toward her. If, however, you were indifferent toward her mood, your energy would remain unchanged. Your need for the other person to be in a specific mood is what drains you. In order to change your situation, evaluate your need to please. Ask yourself, what would happen if you attended to your own needs instead? Would the complainer stop liking you? Do you feel guilty if you are in a good mood and the other person is not feeling happy? What makes you believe that you are responsible for the other person's mood? Are you aware that your concern for the other person is at the expense of wasting your own energy? Whenever you recognize that a situation is disturbing or unhealthy for you, change your attitude or drop any sense of responsibility to make the other person happy.

Another example of having your energy drained by others is when someone constantly requires your attention. This situation reflects that someone's needs are not met and it may be highly distracting and tiring. Like finding a leak in your house plumbing, when you recognize that you are in a situation that causes an emotional leakage, you have to, first, evaluate its source, and second, determine whether you can fix it or you need to let someone else take charge. When engaged in a draining relationship, you need to decide who is needy, what the need is, and whether you have the capacity to provide what is needed.

Mel wanted his relationship with his sister to be inspiring for both of them, but no matter what he did, it seemed like nothing ever worked. After their mother died, Mel's sister Melody raised him. They lived together, handling life's chores according to their capacities and skills. Melody was the provider; Mel was the handyman. Melody was the cook; Mel was the housekeeper. Melody was the idea person; Mel was the executor. They were a team complementing and inspiring each other. They lived happily for many years until Mel finished college and moved far away from home and to a big city.

Exposed to new "culture" and surrounded with opportunities, Mel changed his attitudes and found a new enjoyment in life. He wanted to share his success with Melody. He wanted her to recognize his improvement and desire it for herself. Instead, Mel's sister felt that, through his change, Mel had abandoned her. He was caught up in an emotional tug-of-war between the need for Melody to approve the "new" Mel and the desire to continue with his personal growth. Since Melody neglected to notice his excitement, she often criticized Mel's change. At the same time, Melody never missed an opportunity to tell Mel how much she had sacrificed for him. Regardless of how many thanks Mel gave her, it never seemed to satisfy Melody's need. Instead of feeling energized and fulfilled by their relationship, Mel felt drained around his sister. He also guessed that Melody was not happy and that they were both frustrated and emotionally empty.

I helped Mel address this situation one aspect at a time. First, Mel took care of his need for approval. He accepted his change as beneficial to him and as an inevitable part of his personal growth. He no longer expected his sister to understand or approve of his transformation; he just had to feel truthful toward his own uniqueness. Second, we spent time identifying values that Mel gained from his sister so that he could relay his appreciation and gratitude to her. Mel used any given opportunity to recognize Melody's skills and attitudes, and shared his admiration for her. Third, Mel expressed how much he loved his sister and how much she meant to him, assuring her that he would always do his best to help and support her. Mel stopped feeling responsible for his sister's happiness. Instead of being drained by spending his energy to fix her unhappiness, he filled his heart with love and attentiveness, directing his energy to building up his sister's strengths. Instead of holding her up and walking with her, he gave her the shoes and encouraged her to walk on her own.

Interestingly, Mel felt a change in his energy as soon as he adjusted his attitude. He kept reminding himself that his greatest responsibility is to take care of himself. Mel continued accepting and loving his sister, patiently waiting and believing in her capacity to find her own solutions. While it took Melody some time to find her way around, eventually their relationship became inspiring again.

Understanding the performance of your own energy gives you knowledge and authority over your life. You are at the control panel of your energy field, and you have the power and responsibility for its state. With the ability to interpret the information provided by your emotions, you can deliberately influence and manage your own energy level and flow. Instead of being swayed by the "negativity" of a specific feeling, understand its message, and adjust your mood. Instead of being dependent and influenced by other people's energy, identify non-serving behavior and choose to intentionally shift your own inner energy.

Exercise 2
Developing Night Vision

The objective of this exercise is to expand your awareness inward and give you a better understanding of your inner energy. You will learn to recognize physical sensations of inner energy associated with your thoughts and emotions.

Attention is the focal point of your awareness. You can affect the state of your inner energy by shifting your attention. The first part of this exercise will teach you how to turn you awareness inward.

1. Stand on one foot and keep your balance. Bring your attention inside of your body. To maintain your balance, you have to focus and fine-tune your awareness inwardly.

2. Feel the center of gravity for your physical body. Bring your attention to that center. Do you feel your energy centered?

3. Shift your attention outward. Start looking around. Start paying attention to anything else but your inner center of gravity. Are you still maintaining your balance? Oftentimes, when you are distracted, your attention becomes scattered, and you wobble.

4. Regroup and bring your attention inward again. Find a feeling of inner stability. Do you feel in control and your energy centered?

The second part of this exercise will teach you how to sense your inner energy that is, its state and movement. Our inner energy is experienced in two ways: on the outside as being open or closed, and on the inside as "something" in motion. To accomplish this part of the exercise, recall what happens when you enter a dark room. You have to stand still and stay internally open to receive information until your eyes start noticing something. At first, your eyes give you faint images, and you keep accumulating information until you make sense out of them and recognize the objects. Use this same state of mind—open and waiting for sensations to come in during this process. This exercise will feel awkward at first because the sensations I am asking you to feel are unfamiliar. Do not worry; just be curious.

1. Start by bringing your attention to the area around your heart. Imagine being worried. Can you feel your heart area being closed? Where do you feel the "closed" sensation? Now imagine being relaxed and loving. Can you feel your heart area open? Where do you feel the "open" sensation?

Is it in the area of your heart? How far away from your body can you feel the sensation? Write down your observations.

_____

_____

_____

_____

_____

_____

_____

_____

_____

Look at the feelings listed below. Take two feelings, like curious and suspicious for example, and imagine what they feel like. Compare them side-by-side, switching from one feeling to another, and write what you feel. Do you feel open or closed? (For more practice, please refer to table 1 of the "Tables" section.)

Curious _____	Suspicious _____
Excited _____	Anxious _____
Happy _____	Sad _____
Determined _____	Stubborn _____

2. To sense the state of your inner energy, imagine the inside of your body being a pool filled with water. Imagine feeling ashamed. Can you feel the water sinking? Now imagine being angry. Can you feel the water boiling and rising? Look at the emotions listed below, imagine what each emotion feels like, and write down your observations. What is happening with the water? Do you feel its pressure or movement? Be curious and creative in your description. (For help or more practice, please refer to table 1 of the "Table" section.)

Anger   _____

                 _____

                 _____

Fear

_____

_____

_____

Pride

_____

_____

_____

Confidence

_____

_____

_____

Disappointment

_____

_____

_____

Hope

_____

_____

_____

Chapter Six
Emotional Literacy: Knowing Your Emotional Buttons

There are two basic skills that everyone must have to function in society: language and math. Imagine being illiterate. If you weren't able to read, you couldn't read street signs, drive, or answer your mail. To be illiterate means to be limited. Illiteracy narrows our scope of understanding and restricts our thinking capacity, limiting our options. On the other hand, imagine not knowing simple math—not being able to distinguish between numbers, to add, subtract, multiply, or divide. Without math, you would not understand time and money; you would not know what time to get up and go to work, what time the stores open or close, how much money you make, or how much things cost. Knowing math facilitates our social structure and interactions. Similar to the way language and math help us to understand and relate in society, knowing the meaning and power of our emotions helps us to engage in life on a personal level. (The next chapter addresses emotional math.)

Learning a language does not happen spontaneously. To know the language, one has to intentionally learn individual words and their meanings—discovering when and how to use them in different contexts. A person is considered proficient in a language when she can use words appropriately to communicate effectively. To be emotionally literate means to be mindful of how we feel in a given situation and to be aware of how our thoughts and actions affect our inner energy and the energy in others. As an excellent writer knows how to use the subtle meaning of words to engage readers emotionally; similarly, we have to be emotionally literate and know how to manage our inner energy so that we can engage in life in ways that bring us joy and fulfillment.

To become emotionally literate, we have to learn to distinguish individual feelings, understand our inner energy, and manipulate it effectively. A father that teaches discipline to his children can be more effective if he pays attention to his feelings and the feelings of his children while implementing the rules. The choice of the words he uses can elicit different feelings in his children and consequently, support or undermine his intention. If he explains the importance of discipline as a personal and social structure that provides *order* and *protection*, his children would more likely comply with the rules. But, if the father demands his children to *obey* his rules and threatens them with punishment, they would probably resist his teaching and demonstrate unwillingness to cooperate.

The better comprehension and command we have of our feelings, the more we can conduct our lives with finesse. When we refer to pushing one's buttons we often think of someone provoking anger, but this phenomenon is not limited to anger only. We can expand the concept of emotional buttons and apply it to other feelings. What would happen if we could take all our feelings and transform them into accessible buttons? At our fingertips, we would be able to motivate ourselves by pushing on curiosity or passion, or take the steam out of fury by pushing on indifference or patience. Hence, knowing how to elicit a desired feeling is transformational and empowering. To be emotionally smart means understanding our emotional buttons and knowing how to operate them deliberately.

Because our emotional brain starts working before our cognitive brain develops, we start out behind in comprehending our feelings. When thinking, our thoughts are clear and delineated, while when feeling, our emotions are vague and intertwined. Our ability to use words to express our thoughts is mature, while our capability to use words to describe our feelings is juvenile. On an emotional level, we often behave like adolescents; we are reactive and not articulate.

In general, we experience complex feelings but process them in a simplified manner. In one situation we can experience various feelings yet internalize them by overlooking their individual values. For example, you meet someone and you feel curiosity because of his charisma, admiration for his academic accomplishments, bewilderment because of his lack of business success, confusion because of his sloppy appearance, and anger because of his condescending comments about less fortunate people. Instead of taking mental notes of your individual feelings and using them to portray a colorful picture of your interaction with the person in question, you rush through the experience and internalize your emotional impression as "okay."

Simplifying our experiences has its advantage and disadvantage. Although simplifying feelings may protect us from being overloaded with information, it can also deprive us from details we may need to make informed decisions. Emotions are messengers informing us about the ways we engage in life, i.e. how we relate and potentially interact with others. When our involvement is simple, a simplified understanding is sufficient, but when our involvement is sophisticated, the messages we receive from our emotions are complex and subtle.

To better understand the complexity of emotions, imagine your feelings as pieces of mail. In your mailbox, you find various envelopes containing different information. To sort through your mail, you have to look at each envelope individually. You cannot summarize the content of every individual envelope by opening only one nor could you be completely sure of its contents until you look inside. It is the same with your feelings. I am not suggesting that you go through every experience analyzing every little feeling, rather I am suggesting that you learn how to access and understand your feelings so that you can retrieve the information as you need or choose.

The purpose of life is in self-discovery and self-expression; emotions are the messengers assisting us in accomplishing our purpose. The more precise we are about distinguishing between our feelings and their messages, the more adept we become in processing them. Because we engage in many situations simultaneously, our emotional experiences overlap, and our feelings are multilayered. Only when we comprehend a wealth of feelings can we engage in life luxuriously. Experiencing life through a scarcity of feelings does not mean that life itself is not lavish. By having limited mastery of feelings, we limit our capacity to develop our potential and to enjoy life fully. Being emotionally literate means having the ability to understand and express the full spectrum of feelings and doing so at will.

Our lack of emotional education shows up whenever we are emotionally upset or troubled. Those are the times when we experience and demonstrate the discrepancy between our thinking and feeling abilities. As we try to interpret complex messages with an immature vocabulary, we find ourselves incompetent. Unsuccessful in expressing our feelings and troubled by our inner handicap, we view our own feelings as erratic and out-of-control. Annoyed with the presence of unclear feelings and puzzled with our incapacity to decipher them, we become internally tormented and angry. Confident about our thinking ability, we therefore doubt—or worse yet, ignore—our sentiment. We start believing that something is wrong with our feelings, when in reality our thinking *method* is erroneous.

Instead of thinking about feelings in a simplified way, we need to expand our emotional vocabulary. When we are knowledgeable about a language, our vocabulary consists of a variety of words, and we know the nuances of their meanings. The way to emotional literacy is to untangle our emotions and to expand our awareness and knowledge of a variety of feelings. The process of clarifying emotional experiences involves increasing both the number and the variety of feelings.

When emotionally flustered you can list as many feelings as possible to describe your state and then branch out from your listed feelings by looking for similar or opposite emotions. The intention of this exercise is to create a new dimension to your emotional experience and, in the process, possibly gain insights into your life. The following example will illustrate how to expand your emotion vocabulary.

Mary called her emotionally confusing state her "weirdness." When asked to provide other feelings that could describe her state, Mary listed "uncomfortable, upset, hurting, and beside myself." To branch out her emotional experience, Mary listed the feelings that she believed were the opposite of those previously expressed. Her opposite-feeling pairs were the following: uncomfortable/comfortable, upset/happy, hurting/happy, and beside myself/content. It often happens that our opposite feelings do not represent logical antonyms, or that we pair one feeling to two or more separate feelings. In Mary's case, the paired feelings of uncomfortable/comfortable stayed the same. The next two feelings (upset and hurting) had the same match (happy), which did not necessarily represent their logical antonym. When one is not hurting she is not necessarily happy, but rather, neutral; and when someone is not upset she is probably at peace.

We then examined her feeling of being beside herself. Mary explained further, "It's like I keep trying to understand what's wrong but can't put my finger on it, which makes me even more beside myself." To gain clarity, we unfolded her feelings by looking for the opposites. Mary and I explored finding the opposite of the opposite until something clicked. The opposite of feeling beside herself, Mary said, was content; the opposite of content was discontent; the opposite of discontent was satisfied; and *satisfied* was the word that resonated with Mary. She was dissatisfied with an event that happened at work that compromised her values and caused her to doubt her choice of careers. The situation at work triggered her feelings, calling upon Mary's attention. Ignorant of their purpose and unable of distinguishing their messages, Mary was indeed feeling weird. By acknowledging her messengers and understanding their messages, Mary felt in control again. Once her emotions were untangled, a new light shone on the problem, and Mary was able to choose a new attitude toward the troubling work situation.

The exercise of acquiring an emotional vocabulary is no different from writing an important note. Usually, when you write, you search for the exact word because you want to make sure that your words depict your feelings with clarity, so you keep writing and revising your message until you hit the right word. In the process, you internally search, testing words by sensing them until you find the word that resonates with your feeling. To expand your emotional vocabulary, you can do the same. Make an effort to be precise about your emotions, articulate your feelings, and keep practicing until you develop the skill of fluent and accurate expression. Always be aware of what you want to accomplish, a feeling you want to experience so that you can monitor your emotional transformation until you achieve your goal.

Jack was sitting at the company's yearly meeting. He had been feeling apprehensive about this meeting for weeks. On several occasions, we talked about his previous experiences, examined what made them unpleasant, and wondered about Jack's expectation for the upcoming meeting. Jack was annoyed and disappointed with previous meetings; he felt criticized by his boss and unsatisfied with results. Jack wanted a specific change to happen but never expressed his ideas or stated his expectations. I suggested that Jack approach the meeting differently. First, he was to look at his boss' comments from a different prospective; instead of receiving comments as an attack to Jack's competence, he was to view them as a compliment to his capacity to handle constructive criticism. Second, he was to view his ideas as helpful to others and that withholding them would be rude and selfish. Equipped with two new points of view, Jack felt enlightened and encouraged, thus less apprehensive about the meeting.

A week later, during our session, Jack was excited to tell me that the meeting went well. Jack realized that his boss was using Jack's division to demonstrate ups and downs, struggles and successes. For the first time Jack heard his boss entirely registering his praise in addition to his criticism. Usually, one part of the boss' comments would push Jack's "unfairness" button and Jack would spend the rest of the meeting internally arguing about the unfairness of his boss and life in general. This time, however, Jack did not assume a disapproving intention behind his boss' comments, which in turn deactivated Jack's "unfairness" button. Instead, he was able to see the big picture and hear the true meaning of the comments expressed during the meeting. I then asked Jack whether he shared his ideas at the meeting and he said: "I opened my mouth."

Interestingly, we often say things unaware of the energy behind our words. I suggested that Jack *feel* the statement he made and try to describe what happened at the meeting differently. I offered three different sentences, letting him compare the way he felt about them. The first sentence was "I opened my mouth," the second "I spoke up," and the third sentence was "I expressed my opinion." After examining his feelings, Jack reported that the first sentence evoked a feeling of insecurity and of not being in charge. He realized that "saying whatever" made him feel more insignificant. The second sentence brought up a feeling of daring, being courageous to express his opinion. He felt openness and self respect. The third sentence demonstrated assertiveness. He felt confident and significant. When I asked Jack to choose the sentence based on his feelings, naturally he chose the third version.

To be emotionally literate means to know the energy behind the words so that we can use our words to produce the effects we desire. As we will discover in the following chapter, knowing emotional math means being able to calculate–and ultimately control–the rise and fall of our emotional energy. When we combine both, emotional literacy and emotional math, we use our emotional intelligence at its utmost.

Chapter Seven
Emotional Math: Operating
Your Emotional Buttons

Learning about emotional math helps us to recognize and understand the dynamics of our inner energy. We all intuitively know how to keep emotional score with people who offend us or who do not show us the level of respect we deserve, but have you ever thought about how you keep this internal score? How do you know the amount of respect you deserve? Imagine if you could do your emotional math intentionally, and take time to clear and balance all your emotional accounts? Wouldn't you feel free and empowered?

Our positive and negative emotions, good or bad feelings, or energy being up or down, are all common expressions we use to describe the experience of inner energy. Understanding emotional math is about giving you the tools to understand and manage your inner energy. It helps you distinguish when your thoughts are dragging you down and when they are empowering you. It helps you recognize what you value as somewhat important vs. very important. It gives you the ability to choose your feelings and gather the information you need to make meaningful decisions. Moreover, it give you control over your life.

Your thoughts, decisions and actions affect the state of your energy. The rules of addition, subtraction, and multiplication that apply to numbers also apply to your feelings. For example, some thoughts, such as thinking about vacation, can add to your enthusiasm, while others, such as dieting, can draw on it; some thoughts bring a manifold of happiness, such as thinking of the person you are falling in love with, while others, such as hopelessness about finding true love, can spiral you into depths of depression. Some decisions motivate you for short periods, such as the New Year's resolutions most people make, while other decisions keep you emotionally committed for a long time, such as deciding to finish college. Understanding what affects your inner energy, i.e. your feelings, is emotional math.

I'm not a scientist, and you probably aren't either, but that doesn't mean we cannot comprehend our energy. The electromagnetic field of our energy expresses itself in waves. Each wave's value depends on its *strength* (a number between one and ten, for example) and *direction* (plus or minus, positive or negative). What we hold as important determines the strength of our feelings. The distinction between a positive and negative feeling is determined whether we are *in,* or *out,* of synch with nature. As previously discussed, the natural tendency of a wave is to be steady and to propagate. Therefore, the tendency of our inner energy is to be stable and expand, and this is what happens when we experience contentment, love, or any other sensation we refer to as a "positive" feeling. The opposite experience occurs when our inner energy feels unstable, blocked, shrinking, or erratic, and we describe our feelings as "negative." Think of two different situations, one that elicits a feeling of confidence, and the other of insecurity. Compare those two states by going back and forth between them. Can you sense how, when confident, your energy is open, steady, and exuding, but when insecure, your energy flow is closed, its pattern irregular, and the "amount" decreases? By recognizing and understanding what makes you feel positive or negative, and thus what makes your inner energy flow and expand or restrict and shrink, you can choose the attitude that is the most beneficial to you.

You already use emotional math unconsciously. You certainly have had experiences when something happened and your inner energy suddenly changed from excitement to fear, or from confidence to insecurity. You have performed emotional math when someone offended you and you evaluated how much suffering the offender deserved, or you made a decision but didn't follow-through because you did not put enough commitment into your decision. All those experiences explain that you are, in some way, calculating your inner energy, manipulating it daily. You just need to understand what it is that you do and how to apply the same rules deliberately.

The following are the rules we need to consider when calculating our emotional math:

1.   Your decisions are always driven by the strongest feeling you are experiencing at that moment. When two waves–i.e. feelings–interact, the strongest feeling wins.

2.   Your overall mood is a sum of many individual feelings. Your thoughts and feelings are intertwined; every though generates a feeling and your overall mood is affected by your thinking.

3. To change your mood, you need a significantly strong feeling. To overturn a wave/feeling that pulls you in one direction, you have to generate a significantly stronger feeling moving in the opposite direction.

4. You can change the polarity of your feelings: positive to negative and vice versa. What you estimate to be important or unimportant places a positive or negative value to your experience.

The first rule explains that at any given moment you feel many feelings but always act out from the most predominant feeling. When two waves combine, their values add or subtract and the strongest wave always wins. If you think thoughts that are supposed to make you feel positive but you are not convinced of their validity, your negative feeling will overpower your positive thinking. For example, you were recently promoted and you are feeling insecure about your new position. To overcome your insecurity, you say to yourself that there is no reason to feel insecure and that you should feel confident about your skills. However, thinking about your confidence is eliciting anxiety. Now in addition to questioning your skills, you are becoming nervous about someone discovering your lack of confidence. In this case, the thinking about being confident did not bring the feeling of confidence; rather, it triggered anxiety and increased your feeling of insecurity. It is important to know that for the "thinking positive" technique to work, you *have to feel* positive. In order to create a change of your feelings, you have to find a thought, situation, or an attitude that can really generate a desired feeling. Only when you have a strong positive wave of self worth can you overpower the negative feeling of insecurity. For example, instead of desiring to feel confident but not believing in your capacity to perform, you may remind yourself of qualities you believe you have, such as creativity and resourcefulness. By remembering your skills and feeling truthful about them, you will experience internal transformation of your feelings from insecurity to confidence.

The second rule explains that your overall mood is a sum of many individual feelings. We interact with our physical and social environment by engaging energetically, for example, we may feel apprehensive and excited about going on a first date. Considering the complexity of our interactions, our inner energy is pulled in many directions and therefore our overall mood, at a given moment, reflects the sum of many individual feelings.

Watching a sunset may not elicit usual joy if you are highly stressed. Your overall mood is the sum of many individual feelings. Every thought and every feeling you have are subjected to an internal count; while you are experiencing things, you are adding and/or subtracting from your overall energy. For that reason, having an optimistic or pessimistic attitude places a plus or minus value to your emotional math and thereby affects positively or negatively your experiences as a whole.

Mathematics is impersonal, so beware of any comments, actions, or attitudes that generate negativity. For example, on occasion, you may make comments to yourself or to others, playing ignorant or stupid and belittling your skills and/or capacities. Although hoping to be humorous and entertaining, your feelings may not match your intention. Whenever you make a joking yet belittling comment, examine your feeling. Do you feel enriched or impoverished by your comments? Are you making comments hoping for others to complement and praise you? Are you hoping to hear them say that you are not stupid, rather smart, or are you really enjoying being witty? Make distinction between a feeling of enjoyment when being clever and funny, and the feeling of self-doubt when making fun of yourself. Over time, your comments, seemingly innocent, can generate significant self-doubt and self-rejection. Remember, the accumulated feelings will affect your overall mood.

The third rule to consider encompasses first two rules of emotional math. A friend of mine was learning to ride a motorcycle. She is a successful business woman, but, being in a new and unfamiliar situation, she started doubting her abilities. The thoughts running through her head were the voices of people telling her that riding a motorcycle is dangerous. Listening to those voices, she became overwhelmed with insecurity and fear, compromising her ability to drive and therefore, her safety. She had to overcome her detrimental emotional state.

To disarm the intimidating thoughts that ran rampant in her head, she created a motorcycle-riding mantra that would evoke empowering feelings. She started reminding herself that she's smart and that she can handle many business situations; therefore, she can make wise decisions on the motorcycle. She kept affirming her capacities, evoking feelings of self-confidence, and building a foundation of security and being in control. "I'm smart, I'm safe, and I can ride" she repeated over and over to herself as she drove carefully down the road. Over a period of time, she was able to create enough positive feelings of security, knowledge, and capability to overpower the old fear-based negativity. To her surprise, riding her motorcycle then became relaxing and enjoyable.

The fourth rule tells us that our perceptions and values determine what we consider positive or negative, desired or undesired. Depending on what you perceive as important or unimportant, you determine a neutral point from which you feel some things as positive and some as negative. You determine the polarity of your feelings according to your own personal standards and you can adjust it at any time. Every individual has a scale of personal values, which is subjectively graded. Everyone's scale has plus and minus values and various degrees of intensity. For example, you may consider a mere acquaintance's behavior as negative, but when displayed by your friend, you may value the same behavior as positive. Conversely, you may consider a specific behavior permissible for others but not for yourself.

Most people have inner chatter, an internal dialogue probably developed to keep us behaving in a socially acceptable manner. To evaluate ourselves, we judge our behavior against a specific set of standards. Interestingly, the measurement scale we use to evaluate ourselves is usually off balance, with a neutral point off center. We often calculate our behavior on a negative side of the scale. With a skewed evaluation technique, it is no surprise that our self-criticism does not elicit pleasant feelings. For example, you and your friend make the same mistake. Your mental attitude toward the friend's action is gentle and forgiving, while toward yourself, it is harsh and unforgiving. Your friend's behavior is evaluated positively and yours negatively. Understanding the distortion of self-criticism can help you adjust your inner measurement scales and judge your behavior by more realistic and congruent values. Whenever engaged in self-criticism, ask yourself whether you are using the same standards to judge yourself as you would apply for someone you love and respect, such as your best friend.

Understanding the movement and behavior of our inner energy positions us at the control panel of our lives; we can choose our thoughts and feelings according to their energy value and we can engage in experiences by calibrating their emotional worth. By performing emotional math and demonstrating our emotional literacy, we are able to fully engage and enjoy our lives.

Chapter Eight
Beware of "Victim" Mentality

Resisting chocolate was the hardest. Chantal was seriously struggling to lose weight. Diet after diet, resolution after resolution, her disappointments over-weighing hopes, Chantal was tired of being obese, but exhausted from fighting extra pounds.

Faced with her favorite pleasure, she would go through an array of pros and cons, looking for the discouragement, yet hoping for the permission to eat a dessert. She would always end up convinced that she deserved to treat herself. Chantal would tell herself that she put up with people at work and made sacrifices at home and that she deserved a reward for her good behavior.

Chantal would eat her treat, then regret her decision and feel miserable. She was disappointed with her lack of strength to resist the temptation, but especially with the unfairness of life. She often denied her wishes in order to please others, but, on occasion, when she wanted to please herself, she would be punished. For having an occasional sweet pleasure, she was punished with a corpulent figure. Chantal would look at herself in the mirror and dislike her appearance, feeling angry and unhappy with herself and her life. Life was just not fair to her.

During one of our coaching sessions, I introduced Chantal to emotional math. We looked at her emotional experiences associated with either taking or refusing, for example, a piece of chocolate. First, we examined her feelings after eating chocolate. The immediate feelings were pleasure, a sense of relief, and satisfaction. The subsequent feelings were disappointment and dissatisfaction. In addition, since Chantal did not like her overweight body, she would also feel self-rejection and disgust. Her immediate positive feelings were short-term and weak, while the subsequent negative feelings were strong and long lasting. By comparing her short-lived pleasure to her long-term discomfort and pain, Chantal realized that the fleeting sweetness of chocolate was soon followed by a lasting aftertaste of bitterness. As she performed emotional math and realized the emotional value of her choice to eat chocolate, Chantal was able to make decisions that were emotionally beneficial to her.

Interestingly, when presented with a choice to give up chocolate and get the figure she desired, Chantal discovered an inner conflict. Although ready to give up chocolate, she was reluctant to give up the feeling she got from eating chocolate. "Rarely do I get to please myself, and chocolate gives me that little, simple pleasure. It is not fair that I have to give up the only pleasure I have," she lamented. Chantal felt that life was unfair because her habit of constantly pleasing others left her unsatisfied and hungry for "simple pleasures."

Disillusioned that others could not like her if she were honest, Chantal had to "behave." For example, she could not rest when tired, or not even postpone cleaning her house, afraid that someone may judge her as untidy, nor could she refuse listening to a colleague's chatter, afraid of hurting his feelings, even thought he would interrupt her in a middle of an important project. Trapped in meeting unfair expectations, Chantal was a victim—not of an unjust society but of her unrealistic beliefs. Not being able to be her true self left Chantal filled with bitterness. Similar to eating a dessert, pleasing others brought her a short-term satisfaction and a long-term feeling of resentment. Furthermore, Chantal disliked her lack of inner strength to speak up her truth, and once again, felt self-rejection.

It was obvious that feelings of resentment and self-rejection were making her emotionally poor. Chantal realized the importance of changing her attitude and intention. No longer a victim, her intention turned to protecting herself from emotionally unpleasant consequences. Instead of pleasing thus favoring others, she became fair to everybody, herself included. Instead of doing or saying what she thought will make her likeable to others, Chantal would behave as if they already liked her, then, she would decide about her intention, and express her truth to strengthen her resolve. She connected her habit of pleasing others to unpleasant feelings of resentment and self-rejection. Instead of following an impulse to be overly nice, Chantal would remember the intense emotional discomfort this behavior caused, which would help her change her attitude. Whether Chantal was tempted to "behave" and please others or "misbehave" and eat something that would compromise her weight plan, she would consider the consequences of her action until she would feel a strong discomfort sufficient to encourage her to act differently.

Whenever Chantal's intention was to change her attitude or achieve her desired body weight, her intentions had to be clear. When we make decisions without a clear intention it is like starting a trip without a clear destination; we can end up any place. Knowing your intention is vital to doing emotional math. Your intention determines your overall state of inner energy.

A useful application of emotional math is in making decisions by anticipating the result. Let's say you want to change a habit. You have to evaluate the end feeling associated with your habit and then find a feeling that you would prefer to feel instead. Compare the two feelings, and make sure that the new, desired feeling is significantly stronger than the undesired one. Once you know your destination, then you can adjust your perception, decisions, and actions to generate the desired feeling.

Attention is the spot where you point your awareness and you place the center of your energy. Intention is the spin—or direction and movement given—to your energy. For example, my attention may be focused on you, but my intention could be to intimidate you and destabilize your energy. More positively, my intention could be to support and encourage you, thereby boosting or soothing your energy. Remember, no matter my attention or intention, you have the final word on the state of your inner energy. I could believe in your abilities and send you waves of praise, but if you keep focusing on your perceived weaknesses, the state of your energy will overpower my influence.

It is the same when someone chooses to focus on negativity; no outside optimism can affect a person's energy until the individual decides to change. If we find ourselves in the company of a pessimistic person, we can share our positive vibrations, but we are not in control of the other person's mood. We can keep our enthusiasm at a desired level, make it visible to the other person, and hope that our attitude will inspire the person to make a different choice, but we should know that we are not responsible for the condition of the other person's energy. Ultimately, you are in charge only of your own mood.

Being ignorant about emotional math, about the ways our energy behaves, makes us reactive. Placed in a reactive mode, we feel attacked and are the victims of our environment. When we understand how energy behaves, we become proactive. We respond to our environment instead of reacting to it. We use our willpower to make decisions deliberately and take charge of our lives. When unaware of the ways energy performs, if someone upsets our energy, our impulse is to produce the same effect in the other person. When others hurt us, we want to hurt them back. This type of behavior reflects the law in physics of action and reaction but bypasses your free will. For the same reason, Chantal's need to reward herself with eating was a reaction to the sacrifices she made by pleasing others. Furthermore, sacrificing her needs to please others is what caused Chantal to feel victimized.

When you understand and are aware of your inner energy, you can use your willpower to adjust your feelings and actions. Instead of unconsciously reacting, you consciously respond. When triggered to react to something, instead of blindly acting, you can use your feelings to reevaluate the situation, do your emotional math, and take care of your own energy accordingly. To practice, you can answer the following questions: What is the state of my inner energy? What is my intention? What do I want to accomplish? Is my attitude aligned with my intention? Is my emotional experience an unconscious reaction or a deliberate response to the situation? What do I prefer to feel instead? What is the decision or action I need to take to generate the desired feeling?

The objective of asking yourself questions is to learn to pay attention to your thoughts and feelings. Doing a good deed should replenish your energy not deplete it, and you need to know the difference. Developing emotional intelligence happens by gaining glimpses of awareness of the movement of inner energy, so be vigilant. Catch yourself when you are making emotionally detrimental decisions, perform your emotional math, and make choices that make you emotionally richer.

PART THREE
Inner Control Panel

Knowing is not enough; we must apply. Willing is not enough; we must do.

Bruce Lee

It's the middle of the night, you are sound asleep, and your house alarm goes off. You jump out of the bed and as you start looking around, you notice that there is a storm outside and as you feel a breeze, you notice your window slightly open. You must have not latched it properly. As soon as you close the window, you make a quick run through your house, assess that everything looks normal, you hurry up to the alarm box, punch in the code and sigh. One minute can feel like very long time.

Imagine a second scenario. You are driving down a road, minding your own business when someone cuts you off. Surprised and scared, your heart starts pounding. You hit the break, and avoid a collision. As you regain the control over your vehicle, anger kicks in. Similar to your house alarm informing you about an intrusion to your privacy, anger informs you about a violation of your standards. You knew how to silence your house alarm, but if you do not know how to silence your anger, it would probably linger with you for the most part of the day. But, what if you had access to an inner control box for your feelings? You would be able to make an assessment of your standards, find the one that was violated, recognize that the danger is over, and deactivate your anger by remembering things that really matter.

Most of us are unaware that we do have an inner control panel for our feelings. We have the capacity to open or close our heart, generate an optimistic mood, or transform a predicament into triumph. We can send and receive love. We can tune into a specific frequency, understand other people's ideas, or feel their pain or joy. We can fine-tune our emotional broadcast and transform anger into determination and boredom into excitement. We can diminish anxiety with faith or increase our peace of mind with honesty. Therefore, we do have many switches and dials that control our sentiment. This segment will teach you what they are and how to use them.

Every time you are in a position to learn about or express yourself, your emotions will inform you about the opportunity. Emotions are like a flashing traffic light calling for your attention. Learn to read their messages so that when your emotional alarm gets set off, you can punch in the appropriate code, disarm your emotional noise, and regain your mental clarity.

Chapter Nine
Willpower: Your Steering Wheal

The *Webster's Universal College* dictionary definition of power is the ability to do or act; and its synonyms are vigor, force, or strength. Applied to our willpower, this definition describes two aspects of human power: one is dexterity, and the other is strength. Dexterity refers to our ability to internally shift and control our will, while strength refers to our capacity to maintain our grip. You can make a decision and stick to it.

The internal control of our willpower is like having an internal steering wheel by which we can manipulate our inner energy. Similar to arriving at a fork in the road, selecting one road, and then turning the steering wheel, we make mental decisions by guiding our inner energy through different options and then internally directing it and committing to one choice. Imagine being indecisive. Can you feel your will going back and forth between choices? Imagine having two objects from which to choose. Visualize them side-by-side and test their value by switching from one choice to the other, paying special attention to the differences in their attractiveness. Now make your choice. Could you sense the subtle shift in your energy the instant you placed your will on the selected choice?

Most people are not aware of the inner sensation that identifies willpower. We exercise our willpower daily, but not consciously or deliberately. You can demonstrate strong willpower in defending your point of view while in the same instant verbalize desperation about your weak willpower to resist indulging in rich food. Ironically, the strength of our will is always the same; only our perception of it changes. When we view an outside attraction as weaker than our inner strength, we sense our willpower as strong; but when the outside attraction seems extremely strong, we perceive our inner power as disproportionately weak.

Remember, in the process of decision making, we select our choices according to our personal standards and personal significance. Our personal significance scale works like an antenna broadcasting our preferences. Whenever we encounter a choice that resonates with our internal measurement scale, we sense a movement in our inner energy. We experience a pulling sensation toward some choices, while other choices can leave us indifferent or even repulsed.

The following example illustrates a misuse of willpower. Janet was twenty-four and dealing with an eating disorder. At the age of eighteen she was hospitalized, and since then she has worked with different professionals on changing her mental image of her body. She was not anorexic at the time we met, but she was very thin. Janet was obsessed with exercising and controlling her food portions. Because Janet did not want anyone to see how little she ate, she always ate alone. Hiding from friends and family, she felt lonely. Janet's problem was not her body image, but her need to feel powerful and in control. By giving her options to exercise her willpower through meeting different challenges (other than counting calories), Janet found new ways to meet her need for power and control. Instead of running and obsessing over burned calories, she started playing soccer and focusing on the game. I also pointed out to Janet that her desire to control her weight was dictating her lifestyle. Janet realized that her choices isolated her from family and friends and that she had to learn to make better decisions that were more beneficial to her. She learned to reevaluate her decisions according to their intent, whether they were productive or unproductive. Janet created a list of her personal values and learned how to make decisions according to those values. For example, if a friend invited her for lunch, Janet was to make a decision according to what she valued more—spending time with a friend sharing anecdotes, laughing, and feeling good, or eating alone, maintaining a certain size, and feeling in control. Janet also had to learn to use her willpower to overcome her obsession and to stop making repetitive detrimental decisions. She developed a mental exercise of questioning her decisions as to whether they were productive or unproductive to determine whether she was exercising willpower or stubbornness. Whenever she was obsessively focused on running or counting calories, Janet recognized her stubbornness and changed her attitude.

As we change our inner values, our attraction to different choices adjusts accordingly. Imagine going to a store to buy a shirt. Some shirts would appeal to you more than others, attracting your attention. The choices that seem the most valuable attract your energy the strongest. Deciding is easy. Now imagine that you are debating whether to spend money on the shirt. Your choices to buy or not to buy are pulling you in opposite directions. In this situation, deciding is more difficult and requires the use of your willpower. The decision you make depends on the intensity of the feelings associated with each choice. If you are unaware of your thoughts and feelings about each choice, then you may choose to compare unrelated values and consequently make a regrettable decision. Let me give you an example.

Imagine that you are on a tight budget and you know that buying a certain shirt would create financial strain. Nonetheless, the shirt is really appealing to you. You think of all the challenges you've faced and about how much you have suffered from the strain the budget is putting on you. You feel tense. Perceiving that being on a tight budget is punishment and causes unfair suffering, you rationalize that buying the shirt is a reward, well-deserved fairness, and a way to relieve your inner tension. You opt for the shirt. So, you make a decision to spend money, influenced by your need to be without the tension. The purchase provides you with the instant relief of your inner tension.

Now imagine that you consider another perspective: you envision yourself with money saved and your financial situation improved. You feel pride. Perceiving your tight budget situation as temporary, you look at the decision about the shirt as an opportunity to exercise your discipline and inner strength. Determined to improve your finances, you make the decision to pass on the purchase. You realize that buying the shirt would create more financial stress, while passing on the purchase will indirectly release your tension. Guided by the same need to relieve inner tension, yet using different standards to evaluate your strain, you make two different decisions. The attraction you feel toward various choices reflects the standards and values that you are aware of in the moment of deciding. While not buying the shirt in the previous situation was difficult, making the same decision from this new place of awareness is easier and more rewarding. The key element in evaluating choices is to identify the choice that would make you the most proud of yourself. In this example the key question is, which values are driving your decision?—getting a compliment and feeling pretty, or being financially responsible and feeling proud?

Because of our lack of knowledge and awareness in the process of choosing, we often overlook the values that we should take into consideration when deciding. In order to use the least amount of willpower and make decisions most effectively, we need to consider the values that are the most meaningful to us. For this reason, it is important to be aware of our unique affinities in order to know what is meaningful to us.

Nathalie had finished law school, had taken the bar exam, and had already started working in a prestigious law firm when she realized that the choice of profession she made was her father's choice, not hers. Practicing law was not engaging her heart. She felt stressed, depressed, and, most of all, emotionally confused. After Nathalie and I examined her situation, she discovered her passion for healing people and went back to school to become a chiropractic doctor. Although she runs a busy practice Nathalie is happy.

When the standards we use to evaluate our choices are congruent with our values, then our attraction to choices is manageable, and making decisions requires less effort. But when our standards are incongruent with our values, then our perception of the importance of certain choices is distorted. We feel strongly attracted to conflicting choices, and we experience inner struggle. In other words, when our values are out of line, our willpower seems ineffective. The defect of our willpower lies in our perception of it, not in its strength. Remember, the power of our will is constant; only our perception of it changes.

Learning to make decisions that are different from those we have made in the past requires time and practice. Imagine driving a car while approaching a crossroads. You are turning left because on the left is the road you have always taken before. To choose this road is easy; its path familiar. However, it is also limiting because the end of the road is predictable. Alternatively, you could take the road on the right. Its destination is not as clearly marked and you have to envision it. To choose that road for the first time, you have to be mindful of its existence and you have to adjust your hold on the steering wheel, especially since you have the habit of taking the old path.

Just as when you drive and realize that you have passed the crossroad and have to back up, you can learn to do the same thing with your decisions. In decision-making terms, if you do not make the preferred decision at the beginning, you mentally return to the deciding process and make a different choice. Subsequently, when you are aware of your choices, every time you find yourself at a decisional crossroads selecting becomes easier.

Returning to the previous example, in which you developed a habit of impulsively spending money, just to regret your decision later is like continuing to take the path on the left. By becoming more emotionally aware, you recognize the unpleasant feeling of regret and stress caused by increased financial strain, which helps you readjust your personal significance scale. Now, at the crossroad of spending or not spending money, choosing the path that brings you short-term discomfort but long-term comfort becomes an easier choice. Reconsidering the purchase of the shirt, returning it, and choosing to save instead of spend represents your new path.

It is important to mention here that if making choices did not require any effort, then the "power" portion of willpower would be pointless. Taking ownership of the power of our will requires understanding the forces of our inner struggles.

Our willpower has no flaws, so we do not need to improve it by building its muscles. The idea of building the strength of one's willpower by resisting temptations implies that there is an imperfection or a flaw in our willpower that needs improvement. In the times that we experience inner weakness, it is not our willpower that is feeble; rather, the importance of temptation is disproportionately high. If we perceive whatever is tempting us as insignificant, there would be no temptation. The word *temptation* implies a choice that, although favorable, is not in our best interest. Therefore, we could look at the appeal of temptation not as a test to our willpower, but as an opportunity to demonstrate our ability to decide. Remember, the more aware you are of your uniqueness—your personal standards and values—the easier it is to make decisions.

For a few years, I used smoking to alter my feelings. Unhappy with my life situation and powerless to change anything, I felt deprived of enjoyment. Having little power to obtain the things I desired, smoking somehow became my enjoyment and reward for my "emotional suffering." Aware that smoking was not good for my health and unsatisfied with the aftertaste of cigarettes, I would often make the decision to stop smoking.

My resolutions never lasted long, however. Failing in my efforts raised guilt and frustration over my weak will. In addition, I felt trapped in a vicious cycle; smoking would provide me with an instant sense of control, but immediately after smoking, I would feel weaker and more out of control. My willpower was in a tug-of-war. I felt guilty because I promoted a healthy lifestyle in my profession, but I was doing something contradictory to my professional and personal values. In addition, I felt injustice because I could not do what I wanted … until I accepted what I *really* desired.

I wanted to feel proud, confident, and satisfied. My temptation wasn't the act of smoking, but the power to choose. I was addicted to the feeling of "being in charge." Because of my unhappiness with my life situation, my self-esteem was low, causing me to feel powerless. The lower my self-esteem, the stronger the need I felt to smoke. Instead of smoking, sticking to my decision to stop smoking became the way to personal control. Instead of selecting cigarettes, conflicting values, and an increasing feeling of personal misery, I imagined feeling proud and confident by demonstrating my inner strength and integrity. Whenever I felt the desire to smoke, I compared the image of myself as a weak-willed person, hiding my dissatisfaction behind smoking, to the image of myself as a strong-willed person, facing my problems and finding solutions. My attention shifted from the desire to smoke to the desire to feel good about myself, and the temptation and inner struggle significantly diminished. Once able to expand my thinking, I discovered other options, and realized my power to choose. As a result, my feelings automatically changed.

Using your will deliberately is powerful. Making decisions with awareness and integrity is empowering. Whenever you are torn between choices or you question your willpower, remember that you are being presented with an opportunity to make congruent decisions. When you remember what is truly important to you, choosing according to your personal standards and values becomes natural and almost effortless.

Chapter Ten
Working Your Inner Switches and Dials

Our energy is our aliveness, our attitude, our spirit. We may not be able to see or understand our spirit, but we are capable of sensing it. In the same way, we may not see or fully understand the air that surrounds us, but we can definitely feel the wind blow. By paying attention to internal physical sensations associated with our emotions, we can comprehend our capacity to control and manipulate our inner energy, and thereby affect the way we feel.

Since we are individually responsible for our own energy, we have the power to turn *on* and *off* our energy field. Do you remember a time when someone offended you and you "closed your heart"? No matter how much the person tried to apologize or please you, she could not reach you until you forgave her, chose to turn on your heart, and open your energy field again. Our sentiment has many switches; hence, we can be *selective* about our feelings. In a job interview, you can keep your insecurity inside and openly display your enthusiasm, while in negotiation you can exhibit some interest, while intentionally hiding your excitement. Besides opening and closing, we can also internally *hold on to* our energy. You can hold on to resentment, and let go of fear. On occasions when everyone else is expressing doubt, you can hold on to your dreams, keep the inner "grip" on your faith and beliefs, and direct your passion to fuel your actions. This capacity proves that we are in control of our feelings.

Furthermore, we have a myriad of dials that control our sentiment. To better understand our capacity to operate these dials, let us examine the way we experience our emotions. Emotions are not disorganized or random occurrences, but strikingly similar to water. This similarity is not a coincidence considering that 70 to 80 percent of our body is made of water. Many behaviors that water displays are comparable to the way we experience our feelings and, thus, our personal energy. Interestingly, we have an awareness of the ways water behaves but are not aware of our feelings.

1. The touch of water can be light or forceful, as when feeling bliss or anger. Water can be calm or restless, and we too can feel peaceful or anxious.

2. Water can *transform* its state; it can freeze or evaporate, or remain fluid. Likewise, humans can transform their attitudes. We can change indifference into compassion, insecurity into confidence. We can take in someone's compliment, apply it to our self-esteem, and alter our level of security. We can make a decision to run a marathon, feel strongly about it, and thereby focus our energy on vigorous training. We can transform indecisiveness into commitment, boredom into excitement, lack of confidence into determination, or weakness into strength.

3. Water exhibits *waves*, and so do we. Like waves, your feelings propagate and affect others, and vice versa. You can display and disseminate anger or happiness, let other people's anxiety or fear influence you, or you can inspire others with your optimism and encouragement.

4. According to the principles of physics, waves can synchronize or clash. Human energy waves can also synchronize or clash. When two waves synchronize, their values combine. When moving in the same direction, two waves can become one stronger or steadier wave, just as two people on the "same wavelength" can enhance each other's lives. Working on a project with a like-minded person helps you accomplish your task more quickly or to a higher quality. In contrast, if two waves are clashing; one wave is going in one direction (positive value), and the other wave is going in the opposite direction (negative value), the resulting wave will be the net result of the two waves. Whichever wave is stronger will determine the resulting direction. Our emotional struggles are nothing more than clashing emotional waves. Imagine a friend who, feeling sad and lonely, invites you over for dinner. You just got home from work and you are physically, mentally, and emotionally tired. You have two emotional waves clashing: one is the desire to help and please your friend, the other is to attend to your own need for rest and quiet. Depending on your evaluation of whose needs have higher importance—your friend's needs or yours—the resulting wave will determine your decision and the direction of your action.

5. Water has the capacity to accept disturbances yet *maintain* its calm state. Water can receive a ripple yet remain essentially undisturbed. You also have the capacity to absorb your emotional waves and remain internally unruffled. In the same way that you can receive an emotional insult and "keep your cool," you can also stay calm when someone pushes your buttons. Sensing irritation or anger building, you can remain composed by keeping yourself emotionally disengaged. You can recognize when someone is trying to provoke you, trying to disturb your energy field, or trying to affect your attitude, and view the situation as someone merely throwing pebbles into your water. You have the capacity to let the disturbance of your energy dissipate by being an observer. At any moment, you can keep your calm. In the human experience, we call this state patience. A Zen proverb says that if in anger you are patient for just one moment you will avoid a hundred days of sorrow.

6. The energy of water goes unnoticeable while dormant, yet demonstrates tremendous power when in motion. Our inner energy is also unnoticeable until someone pushes our buttons. Our emotions demonstrate the dormant potential of the human spirit. Passion and anger are the flip sides of our hidden power. When water moves in an orderly manner and its energy is harnessed, it can power an entire city; but, when its motion is untamed, water can destroy everything in its path. Passion can fuel dreams and inspire great accomplishments. Conversely, a thunderclap of anger can destroy the best of relationships. Faith can generate one's healing power and cause miraculous recovery from illness. Conversely, grief can erode one's heart and lead a person to death.

7. Water builds up pressure against an obstacle. Stubbornness and resentment are examples of feelings that parallel this behavior of water. Just as water builds up against a dam, in stubbornness your energy pushes against someone's opposing opinion or action. In resentment you consider someone's behavior or opinion unacceptable and you hold your energy up against that person. Interestingly, we use the expression "to hold it against someone."

8. Water takes the shape of its receptacle; likewise our energy takes the shape of our personalities. Our decisions and attitudes shape our character and consequently influence our energy fields. The ways you choose to approach situations not only characterize your personality but also define your personal energy. For example, approaching the same

project, you can let your energy dissipate by being scatterbrained, you can wonder and worry about what may happen, or you can make your energy focused by feeling resolved and by keeping your attention on the task at hand. When you decide what your attitude will be, you send out vibrations echoing your uniqueness, projecting your personality "shape." Because you can manipulate the outside layer of your energy field, you can also project whatever attitude you desire. You can display certain characteristics and thereby affect other people's perception of you. It is important to mention, however, that when you pretend to be someone else, your inner stability weakens. Hiding your true self and constantly maintaining a fake image is hard work. Therefore, it takes less energy to be your true self than to pretend. Can you remember a time when you tried to be someone else and you were discovered? Do you remember what it felt like? You probably felt embarrassed. Perhaps the feeling resembled the sensation of water draining suddenly?

9.   Like water circulating, our personal energy can *flow* in many directions. It can flow in, as when you feel admired by someone, or it can flow out, as when you feel admiration for someone. Like a tide, your energy can go up in joy and down in sadness. Comparable to an unsettled stream, you can feel impatient and restless, or you can have a steady flow of energy, as when experiencing compassion or honesty.

10.   Water abides by the principle of *osmosis*—the tendency of fluids to pass through a membrane in order to balance the concentration on both sides. It is interesting that we use the word *osmosis* metaphorically to explain the human tendency to learn in a gradual manner. Similar to the process of osmosis, we can unconsciously absorb and assimilate new knowledge or skills. My mild-mannered friend Elizabeth once shared a house with a sharp-minded (and sharp-tongued) former county prosecutor named Shaun. Given the difference in their housekeeping standards, friction was inevitable. Usually, Elizabeth just cleaned up the messes and, not voicing her discontentment, grumbled silently. Shaun however, liked to vigorously argue his case. One day when Elizabeth returned home, weary from an exhausting day at the office, she was met with just one pile of dirty dishes too many. Like a long-smoldering volcano, she finally blew. Her patience gone, she questioned Shaun in a rapid-fire, accusatory manner: "Are these your dishes? Did you plan to wash them this evening? Answer the question: yes or no!" Knowing well

that Elizabeth had never attended law school, Shaun stared at her in astonishment and then wondered out loud, "Who taught you how to prosecute?" And with a look that was equal parts pride and horror, he realized that he had. The process of osmosis also explains what happens to "good" people when in "bad" company: their initial qualities and skills become outnumbered by assimilated erroneous beliefs and inappropriate behaviors. Furthermore, we can use the process of osmosis to explain how a make-believe attitude can help us grow spiritually. If you want to accomplish something but you are afraid, you can adopt a courageous attitude and allow confidence to permeate and give you the energy to tackle your challenge. This phenomenon also explains why your beliefs and feelings determine how far you will go in life.

11. Like no other liquid element in nature, water freezes from the top so that life below can survive. (All other elements that can appear in both liquid and solid states have a solid state that is heavier than the liquid state, solidifying from the bottom up, which, if applied to ice and water, would extinguish much of the life on earth). Like water, your feelings can be numb on the surface, leaving you emotionally disengaged from your environment and just going through the motions of life, yet you are still alive underneath. We can observe this phenomenon in the example of parents who stay married for the sake of the children, or a person who views work as a job rather than as a vocation.

To understand our energy it is important to mention that our power to control our energy is a function of our will, which lies uniquely within ourselves. Individually, we have the power to manage our own energy pattern; our will can shape our attitude. We can detect a state or a change in our energy field, such as sensing internal calmness or agitation. We can generate or modify our own wave pattern, such as deciding to be in a good mood. Last but not least, we can affect another person's energy field, but ultimately, we cannot control or be responsible for energy fields other than our own. Although we may trigger a wave of change in someone else, we cannot manage what happens afterward. We are responsible for our own energy, and consequently, others are responsible for theirs. No matter how much influence we exert on someone, that individual can always decide what happens with the emotion-wave within his own field. We can accept, reject, ignore, and amplify a wave, just as we can embrace, refuse, neglect, or intensify one's love. Remember, no one can make you feel anything without your consent.

You are the captain of your life; you just need to take charge of your emotional cockpit.

Chapter Eleven
Deciding: Your Power Button

In everyday life, we are presented with many choices and decisions to make. We are constantly assigning values to and making decisions about our actions or attitudes. Much of the time, we are not even aware that we are making decisions. There are two reasons for this: first, as children we chose our food and toys before we even became aware of our decisions. Second, we would be overwhelmed with information if we made all of our decisions with total awareness. For example, when you get up in the morning, brush your teeth, and eat breakfast, you are deciding only half-consciously when to get up, when to brush your teeth, and what or when to eat. Now imagine the same scenario but with total awareness of every decision you make. What a noisy morning that would be! You would be mentally exhausted before even getting to work.

Making decisions keeps us vitally and socially engaged in life. Unlike animals, humans are not blindly directed by instincts, but rather, are internally guided and thus free to make decisions. For example, in the animal world, when an animal is hungry, instinct drives it to search for food. In the human world, one can choose to follow or ignore the instinct to satisfy our hunger pangs. When we get a message that we are hungry, we use free will to decide whether to ignore, acknowledge, or act upon the message. Therefore, decision making is our capacity to engage or disengage in life, like turning a power button on and off. But how do we make decisions?

Contrary to general belief, decision making is not an exclusively mental process; actually, it is a process of collaboration between thinking and feeling. Imagine feeling indifference. How would you make decisions if you could not feel the difference between your choices? How would you improve or change your behavior or attitude if you could not sense the difference in the quality of experiences? Or, how would you express your opinion if you couldn't feel what really matters to you?

When making decisions, we unconsciously go back and forth between thinking and feeling. Our minds present us with possible choices, and our feelings distinguish between them and indicate which are meaningful to us. Simply put, deciding involves three phases: 1) *perception* (taking in information), 2) *selection* (selecting the finalists), and 3) *choice* (choosing a winner).

Perception is the first phase of decision making. It is our internal interpretation of the external world. Perception is like a mental snapshot of the information perceived by the senses and thereby the mind. We take in information, select relevant data, and then we have a mental grasp of the situation.

Imagine you are in a shopping mall, needing to use a restroom. You start looking around, superficially looking past people, windows, and products (irrelevant data), and you consciously search for hallways, doors, and restroom signs (data relevant to your need). You look left—"snap shoot"—restroom not there. You look right—"snap shoot"—restroom there. Your feelings tell you "target found," and you go about accomplishing your goal. Alternatively, you may find a restroom, but after discovering its unpleasant condition (additional applicable data), you decide to search for another option. As illustrated in this example, actual needs and personal standards are both factors in determining which data is important to the decision being made.

Throughout life, we learn about the world we live in and develop a framework of personal standards that represents our understanding of how everything works and relates to us. When making decisions, we use our personal standards—principles and rules—like filters to sift through the information which is how we end up with relevant data. A person who "keeps up with the Joneses" probably regards "social appearance" and "the opinion of others" as highly valued personal standards. The entire process happens unconsciously, allowing us to process information quickly and effortlessly.

The second phase of decision making is *selection*. The process of selecting refers to a mental exercise of sorting through perceived information, feeling and evaluating the data, and narrowing down the choices. We perform the process of selection according to the importance and worth of the information. Each individual has a unique value system—an internal measurement scale created from the combination of our unique own characteristics, beliefs, and experiences. The choices we make and the consequences we experience make up our *personal significance scale*.

In every choice we make, we measure the information by two criteria: its importance and its worth. We select the importance of the information on a Yes/ No principle; something is either important or unimportant (on or off, like a light switch). The worth of the information is determined by our personal feelings, along a range of values (low to high, like a light dimmer). Through the process of selection, we eliminate information that is not important and keep the information of personal significance to us. Next, we gauge information on our scale of personal worth. Narrowing down our choices, we eliminate lower, less relevant data and keep higher, more meaningful information. After this, we select among the finalists, choosing the one that scores the highest on our personal significance scale.

The personal significance scale is created, often unconsciously, by aligning our personal preferences with the standards and rules offered by society. When two separate people are each deciding to buy a new car, they take different values into consideration in making their decision. They each make their decision by considering their personal needs, measured against their own personal significance scale. One person might consider looks (make and model as prestige factors), comfort, plus the desire to own a new car. The other person, operating from a different personal value system, would factor in price, performance, and durability, in addition to the need to simply replace an old car. Both individuals are making the same ultimate decision—which is to buy a car. Their choice of the car may or may not be the same, but their decision-making process will differ, according to the factors they judge to be significant.

An example from my own life of making decisions based on personal significance occurred during the NATO intervention in Serbia. In 1991, when civil war broke out in former Yugoslavia, I left my native country and moved to Canada, where I became a citizen. While working in the United States, I lived in Montreal and occasionally cooked dinners for my Serbian friends.

One of our dinners occurred ten days into NATO's bombing of Belgrade. My friends were hostile toward Canada and the United States, condemning their unreasonable and manipulative actions to protect the Albanians in Kosovo, and indirectly suggesting the innocence of the Serbian army. Trying to understand both sides of the conflict, I suggested that maybe Serbian nationalists were partially to blame and that maybe there was more to the story. Shocked that I could even think such a thing, my friends rallied against me, calling me a traitor and bitterly expressing their disappointment in me. I was stunned and offended by being accused of betraying our people. Outnumbered and confused by their harsh attitude, I shut up and swallowed my opinion. Our conversation soon ended because it was time to join the demonstration against NATO's intervention. Numbly, I followed my friends, but shortly after we reached the streets of Montreal, I felt nauseated and went home.

Saddened and disgusted with myself because I did not stand up for my beliefs and values, I could not "stomach" my weakness. I failed to uphold my altruistic values against my friends' idealistic views. Hurt by my friends' accusations, rejected because they didn't try to understand me, fearful of their abandonment, and concerned for my family, I also suffered a major blow to my self-esteem. In addition, I was confused because my adoptive countries, Canada and the United States, were bombing Serbia, my native land.

Torn between my values and my loyalty, the inner conflict was making me ill. My nausea lasted until I was able to sort through my values and act upon them. My first concern was the welfare of my sisters. I wanted to go to Serbia and protect them. But there was no help I could give my sisters except to share the pain with them. I decided that I could provide better assistance if I stayed where I was and prepared for the future. My second concern was to please my friends so they would like me. Imagining myself agreeing with my friends just so they would like me made me more nauseated, indicating a wrong decision. More important than their liking me was for me to like myself. I realized that my friends were just as scared for their families as I was for mine; we just coped with the situation differently. I acknowledged their attitude and thereby demonstrated my values of tolerance and respect. Finally, I chose to be productive and helpful, so I signed up to volunteer at the Red Cross. This made me feel like I could help make others' lives easier. I accepted my friends' approach and hoped that they would accept mine. I understood their behavior but chose my own, guided by my highest values.

The third phase of decision making is *choice*. Because the process of decision making depends on what we use as a measurement for selection, we have to be mindful of keeping both our personal standards and personal significance scales up-to-date. We go through life collecting beliefs, which become filters forming a framework of our standards and values. The key word here is *collecting*. We accumulate beliefs and carry them around, allowing old beliefs to clutter our present decisions. For example, as an adult, you may desire to further your education. But because your third-grade teacher once told you you were not smart, you doubt your intelligence, so you decide not to pursue it.

Imagine if you never cleaned your closet and kept everything you ever owned: clothes, shoes, toys, newspapers, souvenirs, and more. How encumbered and cluttered life would be! It would be difficult to find, much less maintain, anything that you currently wanted. For the same reason, we should periodically go through our standards and values with the intention of clearing our heads of beliefs that are no longer useful or meaningful.

You can only make decisions in the present; your actual power to decide exists in the here and now. The past and future relate to your choices but not to your power to choose. Accordingly, our personal standards and values—that is, the principles and significance scales we utilize in the process of deciding—should also reflect the present. Our past experiences provide nothing more than a yardstick to measure our growth. What you value today should be a reflection of the current you. When I was in my twenties, staying at home was boring, and going out to clubs was very important; now that I am in my forties, spending time at home is incomparably more valuable than going out to clubs and bars.

Most personal problems we encounter today stem from beliefs with mismatched or conflicting values. When your personal standards and personal significance filters are misaligned, you are left with a double standard—for example, believing that desiring money is evil while at the same time believing that not having money is wicked, too. Conflicting beliefs cause feelings of confusion, along with contradictory behaviors and attitudes. A significant number of people have a double standard about helping others. When they provide help, the act gives them pleasure and enjoyment, but when someone offers help to them, they perceive the same act as a disturbance. Eager to offer help but adamant about refusing it, they display a double standard. If providing help brings pleasure in one person, then wouldn't receiving help offer the opportunity for someone else to experience pleasure?

In the end, you may wonder about the purpose for such a detailed description of the process of decision making. The reason is that the process of decision making affects every area of your life. The decisions you make determine the quality of your life. To control the outcome of your decision making process, you have to understand the steps involved. Only when you know the elements affecting the process can you adjust them and make deliberate decisions. You can try to undo wrong decisions, recognize your missteps, and make better decisions the next time around. You can recognize that when you are about to make a detrimental decision, you should backtrack your selection process, consider different choices, apply relevant personal standards and values, and then make a decision that is most beneficial to you. Decision making is a complex process, but it is also a powerful tool we own. It would be a personal waste to have this sophisticated, powerful machine just to use it haphazardly.

Exercise 3
Sorting Emotion-Mail

The objective of this exercise is to help you gain awareness of the connection between your feelings and your decisions. Remember, emotions are messengers, like mail sent to you. When you sort through your mail, you have to look at each envelope individually. So, always start with identifying one feeling a time. Develop a three-step routine as follows:

1. Receive your messenger

2. Read your mail

3. Choose your response

Since going through your emotion mail is a concise and quick process, the following questions are designed to help you process your thoughts, feelings, and decisions. Considering that you are getting ready for managing emotions in the future, you will use an example from your past for practice.

1. Remember a situation in which you made a decision and regretted it. Write down what the situation was.

_____

_____

_____

_____

_____

_____

_____

_____

2. What were the feelings informing you that you did not enjoy the consequences of your decision? List at least three feelings and write them down.

_____

_____

_____

_____

_____
_____
_____
_____

3. Replay the thoughts that preceded your decision and write them down. Pay special attention to the way you made your choice. Which of your values led you to make that particular choice?

_____
_____
_____
_____
_____
_____
_____
_____
_____

4. What did you feel just before you made the decision? List at least three feelings. What was the meaning/message of those feelings? (For help refer to table 3 of the "Tables" section.)

_____
_____
_____
_____
_____
_____
_____
_____
_____

5. Now that you know the consequences of your decision, how did your perception of the situation change? Can you see that you had more choices than you realized at the time? Write down the old and the new perceptions.

_____
_____
_____

_____

_____

_____

_____

_____

_____

6.   Knowing what you know now, what would be your preferred decision?
     What criteria would you take into consideration to make a new deci-
     sion? Write it down.

_____

_____

_____

_____

_____

_____

_____

_____

_____

Chapter Twelve
Beware of Numb Feelings

Mark was working in his father's business. He had invested mind, heart, and soul into work, hoping to be a partner in the business one day. Unfortunately, his dream had yet to come true. Caught between his love for the business and the hope for his dream to materialize, Mark spent twenty years working for his father only to realize that he may never become a partner as he had hoped. Approaching his fortieth birthday, Mark started questioning his choices.

Mark never felt appreciated and respected by his father. His father was the authority and very controlling of the ways he ran the business. Whenever Mark ventured out to do something to improve the business, he was either criticized or someone else took credit for his idea. Always hoping for an opportunity for the situation to change, Mark grew older and weary from disappointments and frustration. Besides dissatisfaction with his life, Mark also felt angry with his father and, at the same time, guilty for his anger.

Mark was raised with strong family values. As much as he respected his father and his authority, Mark also wanted to be treated as an equal. He was a responsible and dependable adult, and Mark believed that his father should have already recognized him as a valuable partner. Unappreciated for his dedication to the business, his creative ideas, and his people skills, Mark was desperate and emotionally hurting. Although he loved his father, Mark was unable to feel that love. His anger and disappointment were overwhelming.

With no other choice known to him at the time, Mark unconsciously numbed his feelings. Partially to protect himself from hurting and partially to hurt his father back, Mark adopted a careless attitude about his work. Unconsciously, he transformed his dedication into indifference; his profession became a job that he would attend physically but not emotionally. With this new attitude, the things that used to make him upset no longer had an effect on him.

Mark thought he had the situation resolved, but then something else started happening. He started feeling dissatisfied with other areas of his life, he felt trapped and hopeless. Most disturbing to him was that he dreaded going to work.

Being emotionally numb, he lost touch with his creativity and passion. Without his feelings to guide him through self-expression and self-realization, life for Mark had no flavor or meaning. Until he came to see me professionally, Mark did not realize that being emotionally numb does not lead to better emotion management.

The solution to Mark's problems was not to numb his feelings, but to understand their messages and respond to them accordingly. As we began to peel back his layers of indifference, Mark saw that he had misinterpreted his father's attitude. Not being promoted to business partner, Mark felt devalued and rejected, which furthered his insecurity. Instead of being reactive, Mark had to learn to be assertive and proactive. To do so, Mark had to learn about himself first.

When I asked Mark about his skills he answered that he was creative and resourceful in making the business thrive and that he was a good manager and people person, but his voice did not demonstrate confidence. Because of his father's negative comments, or lack of positive ones, Mark felt insecure about his skills and his value as a person, and was therefore obsessively seeking his father's approval. The more Mark needed the approval, the more insecure and vulnerable he was to rejection and disappointment. The more he was emotionally hurting, the angrier he became. A vicious cycle ensued; his feelings escalated and became overwhelming, which caused Mark to opt to numb his feelings. Understanding the cause and the symptoms of his emotional pain was the first step in solving Mark's problem.

Blindsided by his anger and frustration, Mark failed to see the true purpose of work—an opportunity to express and demonstrate his skills. Giving him the option to change his job by imagining other possibilities, Mark realized that he really liked his work but just missed the enjoyment he used to feel. Instead of seeking outside recognition, Mark had to identify his skills and validate them internally. He needed to make a list of his unused skills and write down the feelings that those skills provided for Mark. He also wrote down a list of standards and rules of behavior that he and his father needed to implement to foster a healthy work environment.

After making these lists, Mark was to decide what he needed from his father in order to express his skills. Instead of waiting for permission or approval, Mark was to be assertive, clearly communicate his needs, and persevere until they were met. Mark was to approach his father with these requirements one at a time.

Once Mark stood up for his standards and values, he felt valued and respected. By focusing on his skills, he felt emotionally engaged, alive, and happy again. Although his father did not change in his ways, Mark's attitude changed significantly. Proud of his accomplishments, Mark stopped craving his father's approval.

Mark learned that while protecting himself from unpleasant feelings, he had diminished his capacity to feel at all. The purpose of emotions is not found in how pleasant or unpleasant they are to experience. Their function is in the messages they provide for us. Emotions tell us about our perception and attitude and reveal the ways that we are engaged in life. Mark's feelings of disappointment and frustration, as well as his need for father's approval, were indicating his lack of confidence. Recognizing and utilizing his skills consciously gave Mark a feeling of confidence and satisfaction. Instead of reacting to his father's comments, Mark learned to respond to his emotional messengers. Looking back at his experience, Mark was reminded that numb feelings do not lead to better emotion management. Emotions are personal messengers, and to numb them means to deprive ourselves of valuable information. Numbing your feelings means choosing a bland life. The purpose of emotions is to provide us with the opportunity to understand the ways in which we engage in various situations, to give us the opportunity to use our willpower to choose our attitudes, and to decide how we want to live our lives.

PART FOUR
Emotion Makeover

There cannot be knowledge without emotions. We may be aware of a truth; yet, until we have felt its force, it is not ours. The cognition of the brain must be added to the experience of the soul.

Arnold Bennett

Women are often accused of being *too* emotional and men of not being emotional *enough*. Yet, at times, women can be insensitive and men can be hypersensitive. The truth is that neither men nor women are emotionally centered and masterful; both genders struggle with emotions. We are a highly mentally and technically evolved society, yet in the domain of emotions, we seem to be still living in the Dark Ages.

Feelings play a significant role in the process of decision making; therefore, to understand a gender-specific approach to emotions we have to look back at our history. Taking into consideration the roles men and women played as hunters and gatherers for thousands of years could explain the difference observed between genders and the ways they relate to emotions. Because their tasks were significantly different, men and women used their feelings accordingly. As hunters and protectors of our species, men have used thinking as a primary mode of decision making because in that context, feeling could actually be destructive. They would think, feel quickly, and act. Imagine hunting a deer while listening to every noise, wondering what it could be, fearing danger more than focusing on the prey. This would have been dysfunctional and detrimental to the survival of our species. On the other hand, as gatherers, women have used feelings in the process of decision making differently. While caring for their offspring, women used feelings for non-verbal communication with their children, thus making decisions based on feelings. These habits may explain why women, in general, act more quickly on their feelings than men do and why men appear to be better thinkers than women.

Men and women have an equal capacity to think and to feel, but they use those functions differently. The problem is not in our capacity to feel, whether we feel "too much" or "too little," but that we as human beings are not, in general, emotionally savvy. Instead of using our feelings haphazardly, we need to learn how to use them intentionally and with mastery. To accomplish this, most of us could benefit from a major emotion makeover. We need to invest in changing our ways of seeing and understanding our feelings.

Like thoughts and words, feelings are a form of communication. The purpose of thoughts and feelings is to help us interact with our environment. Without feelings, thoughts are impersonal concepts. Thoughts and feelings function like software that interprets the environment and our relationship with it, providing us with valuable data, so that we can make informed decisions.

Emotional intelligence is our ability to understand, manage, and appropriately utilize our emotions, as well as to understand the feelings of others. Emotional fitness is the degree of agility we have in applying emotional intelligence. The purpose of learning about emotions is to become emotionally smart and gain the ability to transform any aspect of our lives.

Chapter Thirteen
Why Bother?

It's no secret that people struggle with emotionally charged situations. We are thrown into the arena of life unprepared for many of our emotional experiences. With no instructions on how to deal with our feelings, we often face our emotional challenges by inventing coping skills as we go, barely surviving our emotional battles. We are provided with guidance for almost every other aspect of our lives—for example, education, sports, and health. Ironically, for our tough emotional trials we are left to struggle on our own, with no education, instructions, or tutorials. Consequently, we are a highly developed but emotionally ailing society. The constantly increasing number of people demonstrating road rage, depression, sleeplessness, and panic attacks confirms this fact.

Stress is the popular word largely used to describe any emotional strain. For many decades now, researchers have demonstrated, and reporters have told us about the symptoms of stress and its harmful effects on every aspect of our lives; yet we still cannot individually understand or manage our personal stress successfully. Since we already know a lot about the symptoms of stress, the material provided in this book will focus primarily on its cause. Living in a fast-paced society, surrounded with a myriad of stimuli, stress has become our way of living, but it does not have to be our state of feeling. Stress does not always mean distress. A steep roller-coaster ride that causes fear and anxiety can be a highly pleasurable experience for some; while for others, it is a source of disturbance and discomfort. Therefore, it is not the feeling of fear and anxiety that causes emotional strain and suffering, but the way the person internalizes the experience. The objective of learning about emotional empowerment is to gain an understanding of what causes our disturbing feelings, such as stress, and how to transform these feelings into other more preferable emotions.

For scientists, stress is difficult to define because it is comprised of too many variables. Stress is a subjective sensation caused by different situations and associated with symptoms that differ from person to person and that change within each individual. When we struggle emotionally, the problem is not in the type of emotions we experience, but in their overwhelming number and conflicting messages. The cause of stress is strain. In order to feel stressed, we have to experience some internal strain, twist, and tension—an inner conflict of our values and standards. Often subtle in its origins, stress often sneaks up on us. Stress usually represents a potpourri of feelings. The following story demonstrates anger as one of the feelings causing internal stress.

John was eight when his father left home. He still remembers the day when his father found out about his mother's infidelity—the screaming and the drama that led to his father leaving the family. John's father was very strict and intimidating. John's mother was too young and immature to care for children, and she liked to party. Shortly after his father's departure, life for John changed significantly. Both parents found new partners, and John had to adapt to their very different parenting styles. In contrast to John's father, his mother's new partner, Bill, was nice, friendly, and fun. John liked spending time with Bill and dreaded visiting his father—until the day Bill introduced him to his "secret game." Whenever they were alone, Bill would undress John and play with his genitalia until John would physically hurt and cry. John knew something was not right, but he did not know what to do about it. Except for playing the secret game, spending time with Bill was fun. The game was making John uncomfortable and causing him physical pain. John wanted it to stop, but Bill wouldn't listen to him. Deep inside, John knew that if he said something about the game to his mother, she would have protected him and kicked Bill out of their house. John also knew that without Bill to take care of him while his mother was at work, he would have to spend more time with his father, and that seemed even more disturbing and emotionally painful than having to endure the game. Hence, John did not say anything, and he tolerated the situation until Bill and his mother split up.

Now in his late fifties, John sought my professional help because he was incapable of ignoring his anger any longer. He felt stressed and had short temper. His outbursts of anger were seriously affecting his professional and personal life. Over the years, he had tried different therapies and approaches in order to understand and release his problems, from counseling and martial arts to meditation. Nothing helped. John was still filled with anger. John believed that the source of his anger was his childhood experience with Bill. His belief was understandable. John's problem was that he, like all of his therapists, was focused on the act of the "secret game." Since there is no sane person who would approve of playing this type of game, focusing on analyzing the events did not bring about healing for John. The more he thought and talked about it, the angrier he became. Throughout our coaching sessions, I helped John understand that the game itself did not hurt him, but rather the conflicting values that it had left behind.

Looking at John as a healthy adult, I pointed out that what happened during the game did not cause any physical damage or prevent him from being a good father. Even the emotional confusion that the game left behind did not prohibit him from being a successful businessperson. His anger was a messenger asking for John's attention. There were many layers to John's anger. His parents were supposed to protect him, but he was afraid to tell them the truth. Bill was nice and friendly to him, but he also forced John to play a game that made him uncomfortable and cry. John was angry with his father because his father's strict rules and strong voice scared him, so John could not ask him for protection. John was angry with his mother because she could not protect him either; it had been her behavior that caused the family to split in the first place, and she was the person who had brought Bill into their house. In addition, his mother worked long hours, and Bill would take care of John, letting him stay at home and play with his toys. John was angry with Bill because he did not want to stop playing the unpleasant game. Finally, John was angry with himself because he chose to continue with the game rather than tell his parents about it.

Anger is a messenger informing us that someone's attitude or behavior has violated our standards. John's emotional strain was caused by tangled emotions: he did not know which person to trust, he did not know who would protect and who would hurt him, and he did not know what decision to make that would cause the least displeasure. John could not forgive himself for the choice he made to remain silent. He saw himself as weak and submissive, and that image hurt him more then the pain caused by Bill's game.

To help John sort through his feelings, understand their messages, and respond to them appropriately, we had to first address the "secret game." We analyzed various behaviors Bill displayed and concluded that he was a good-hearted person but was mentally and emotionally sick, and we decided that John did not have to deal with him ever again. We also concluded that Bill's game did not physically impair John, so he could let go of the unpleasant memory. Regarding his mother, we decided that she was too young and immature to have effectively cared for children. She was only sixteen when John was born, so most of her decisions revolved around *her* needs. She provided shelter, food, and a relatively stable and predictable family environment, and John was grateful for it. To understand his father's behavior, John imagined what it would feel like being his father's age and having to deal with a highly active boy and an unfaithful teenage wife.

Allowing John to explore the different points of view of the characters in his childhood drama helped him to understand that none of the people involved in the situation behaved with an intention to hurt him. Concerning Bill, John confirmed that in every aspect other than the game, Bill was caring and thoughtful, so John and I decided that we would never understand the sick part of Bill's psyche that needed to play the game. All of the adults involved were only absorbed in their own problems and struggles, thus oblivious to John and his needs. John did not accept their behaviors as permissible, but he was able to forgive them for the confusion and pain they caused. Finally freed from the distraction caused by the anger he felt toward others, we were able to address the most destructive part of John's feelings—the anger he felt toward himself because of the decision he made to remain silent. John thought of himself as weak because he could not speak the truth. He also thought that something was wrong with him because he had chosen to endure a sickening situation.

Judging his decision from the perspective of an adult, the situation provoked feelings of disgust, disappointment, and anger. But, John was only eight at the time. Imagining a boy the same age standing in front of him helped him to comprehend the limited capacity of an eight-year old to fully understand and navigate the situation. Sympathizing with an imaginary boy helped John turn off his judgment and separate his feelings. Children make choices based on avoiding pain, not by considering the consequences. For John, dealing with his father's lack of emotional warmth was the biggest pain he tried to avoid as a child. Once John was able to untangle the complexity of his feelings, his anger subsided significantly. Not only did he learn about the meaning of his anger, John realized how much inner tension and pain was caused by his confusion.

John's story may seem extreme, but it is a great example of what stress is about; a state in which our feelings and values are in a tag-of-war. Our problem is that we do not understand our feelings, so when faced with so many emotional messengers, we became overwhelmed and often "check out" on the surface. Imagine yourself sitting in the cockpit of an airplane. A check light goes on and the needles on some of the dials are moving erratically. What would you do? First, you would establish the purpose and message of each dial, and then you would address the problem, one dial at a time. Our emotions need to be handled in exactly the same way.

Dealing with emotions from a place of ignorance is a struggle, but managing emotions with awareness and choice is empowering. People have been talking about emotional intelligence and our need to be emotionally smart for a while, but for some reason the concept is still not prevalent. Either people do not understand it because they cannot see how emotional intelligence applies to their own lives and therefore they do not see its importance, or they think it's like charisma—you either have it or you don't—so there is nothing you can do about it.

Expressing feelings may be charismatic, but emotional intelligence is more than being attractive or entertaining. Emotional intelligence is about having clarity—the ability to understand and appropriately utilize our feelings as well as to understand the feelings of others. It is our capacity to receive emotional messengers, to understand their messages, and to respond to them intentionally. Emotional intelligence is about knowing the power of emotions and being smart about using the power. This may sound complicated, so let's explore how emotional intelligence can benefit you, one step at a time.

When you are able to understand your emotions as well as the emotions of others you gain the skill to speak lucidly and to hear others with clarity. Mastering your feelings is similar to learning to speak a new language; knowing your individual emotions and their meanings allows you to express yourself and communicate effectively. Furthermore, having the ability to use emotions appropriately and efficiently means knowing their power and impact on your inner energy, mental intelligence, and health. Your empowering feelings can enhance your knowledge and boost your capacities. The opposite is also true. If you have disempowering feelings associated with your knowledge or skills, regardless of your intelligence or talent, you would appear inadequate. A famous quote by Henry Ford says, "Whether you believe you can do a thing or not, you are right." He did not say whether you *think*, but whether you *believe*, because to believe means to have a feeling of truth integrated into your idea. Being emotionally smart means knowing what your buttons are and how to push them deliberately.

To be emotionally smart, you do have to invest effort into developing your emotional intelligence. Just as with mental intelligence, emotional intelligence has to develop gradually. We are not born with the knowledge of words, concepts, and reasoning ability; we learned it through practice and over years of schooling. The good news about investing in your emotional intelligence is that you are already familiar with most of the emotions and may have a sense of their meanings. You already know what anger means and feels like, you just need to learn how to use the feeling appropriately and productively.

You may still wonder, why bother? You should bother because the things you desire—health, success, and happiness—are the byproducts of being at ease in emotionally demanding situations. Doesn't knowing this make the effort of learning the language of emotions worthwhile?

Chapter Fourteen
Personal Awareness: Knowing
What Motivates You

To be aware means to be both informed and alert. Awareness is a state of being in which we are cognizant of certain elements (that is, their positions, values, or significance). In addition, we are observant and ready to relate to those elements. In a state of awareness a person demonstrates the capacity to see both the big picture and the details within it. When one is personally aware, he understands his personal values and the impact of his decisions. He knows and masters the power he possesses to influence his and other people's lives; he takes responsibility for his choices and makes premeditated decisions accordingly. Personal awareness encompasses four different levels of consciousness: awareness of our individuality, willpower, vital energy, and decision making.

The first level of personal awareness is the awareness of our individuality. While personal awareness encompasses various aspects of being human, the awareness of our individuality focuses specifically on our personality. Human individuality comes as a hidden potential; therefore, in the course of life we are constantly discovering and fine-tuning our awareness of our uniqueness. To really know ourselves, we have to pay attention to our likes and dislikes, our skills, affinities, and idiosyncrasies. We have to be mindful of our evolving personality; we have to know who we were, who we are, and who we want to become.

We are each designed to be a little different than others. To be aware of our authenticity is to have the knowledge of our common and uncommon characteristics, and to accept them. Only when we are at peace with our "oddness" can we embrace who we really are. When I was a child, everyone in my family made fun of me because I would walk through the neighborhood and in fifteen minutes have a report on who did what, when, and how. I was very observant. My skill at noticing changes was misinterpreted. For my family, there was no other purpose for my perceptiveness than to spread gossip. Because I was teased about it, I kept my observations to myself, yet never lost my skill. Needless to say, this skill has helped me tremendously over the years; it gave me the alertness and insightfulness necessary to be a good doctor, coach, and friend.

Some believe that we are fixed products of our genes and the environment, but we are more than that. Without a doubt, our parents, siblings, and the environment influence how much of our uniqueness we express; however, their impact is only partial. Because of their individual uniqueness, people recognize and reflect only isolated, disjointed parts of their personalities. What others see in us and how much of ourselves we see in them are like reflections in a handheld mirror. There is not a single handheld mirror that can reflect a full-sized human figure; likewise, there is no single person—not even a parent or a spouse—who can grasp your entire personality. Understanding this fact can prevent us from wasting our thoughts and feelings in an attempt to be recognized by people who do not share our values or to strive to be totally understood by one person.

The second level of awareness refers to our willpower or the authority we exercise in the process of decision making. Our capacity to deliberately choose the course of our lives makes us powerful, independent, and free. Willpower is a household term that is difficult to explain. The *American Heritage dictionary* definition of the will is the mental faculty by which one deliberately chooses or decides upon a course of action. Unfortunately, this definition does not describe how to recognize willpower. As we explored earlier, willpower is the internal steering wheel by which we can manipulate our inner energy; by turning our inner wheel, we can direct and place our inner energy on a selected course.

Many people are not cognizant of their ability to decide, and because of this, they are restricted in the use of their willpower. The reason we lack awareness for the process of decision making is that we start making decisions far before we comprehend our choices. Most often, having restricted options misleads us to believe that we have limited power. Children, as well as some adults, believe that they have no power to choose because they cannot have the choice they want. Deprived of something specific they desire, they become mad or sad—ignorant to recognize that their emotional reaction is a choice, a choice of attitude. To claim our personal power, we need to improve our awareness of our willpower and understand the role it plays in decision-making.

Tom wanted everyone to know that he was an independent man who makes his own decisions. What Tom did not realize was that sometimes his decisions were not *his* decisions. If his spouse or his boss would suggest a new way to approach a specific task, Tom would make sure not to follow the suggestion but to act "independently." His independent action meant that he would resolve to do something different or opposite from what was suggested. Tom was so committed to his "independent" actions that he would often neglect to evaluate his own desires. Tom thought nobody was controlling him; but ironically, by resisting others, his decisions were not self-generated, but entirely dictated by those around him. Unaware of his will power, Tom was using effort to resist others instead of using his will to make deliberate choices.

The third level of personal awareness is the dimension of our inner energy. The presence of inner energy qualifies our aliveness, while our thinking and feeling serve as the internal navigating systems helping us to sustain life. Our feelings signal us when we are hungry or tired, and our mind interprets the messages of our feelings and helps us to determine an appropriate action. A feeling of boredom tells us that our spirit's vitality is wilting, asking for a change that will ignite the spark of life. In a similar way, a feeling of stress informs us that our energy field is scattered and strained, and that if we do not take action to collect and harmonize our energy, our "human system" could break down. Comprehending and responding to our emotional messengers is critical to maintain our optimal liveliness. Accordingly, in order to have a successful, healthy, and fulfilling life, we have to pay attention and be mindful of our inner energy.

There are three focal points of our inner awareness, three areas in which we sense our personal energy: mind, body, and spirit. These three areas are interconnected and can influence each other. A wave generated in one are can propagate into the other two. For example, spirit-generated stress can unfavorably affect one's capacity to think and, in addition, cause a decline in the immune system. Likewise, a person's optimism can physically energize him and inspire his mental creativity. You could be extremely physically and mentally tired but feel instantly reenergized by seeing the smile of a person you love.

Just as our energy can spill over and one area can regenerate another, these, mind, body, and spirit areas can collapse and drain each other. When a change of energy happens in one area, it will probably transmit to the entire system. Imagine working on a home improvement project, feeling energized, creative and proud, when your spouse sees your project and makes a comment that unleashes a cascade of doubts in your mind. All of a sudden, you think about redoing the project, feeling confused, overwhelmed, and drained, with no energy left to continue working on the project. A ripple of doubt in your mind deflated your entire energy state.

Because of the fluidity of our inner energy, we have to raise our personal awareness of its state and movements. Once we understand the phenomenon of our inner energy, its three areas and the way they interact, we gain the ability to engage in life in the most effective way. Similarly to driving a car in the fifth gear, in which the car uses the least amount of energy and runs the most efficiently, we can deliberately make choices that result in a state of personal energy that is more empowering and efficient for us.

With the awareness of the state of your inner energy and the capacity to manage it, the scenario described earlier could evolve quite differently. Realizing that your spouse's comments had a destructive effect on your energy, you could decide to take action. You listen to your emotional messengers, concluding that feelings of self-doubt and insecurity are counterproductive to your desire and intention to finish the project. You evaluate your spouse's "expertise." In this area, you either discover validity in his comments and reevaluate your project, or decide that he is not an expert on the subject and let the effect of his comments dissipate. Either way, you pull your shoulders back, put a smile on your face, and generate a wave of determination and confidence. Your energy comes up, and you are ready to focus on your project again.

Finally, the fourth level of awareness is for our decision making. Since we start making decisions as infants, many times we are unaware of what motivates us to make certain decisions. Educated to believe that deciding could be an exclusively mental process, and thereby untrained to pay attention to our feelings while making decisions, we act (or react for that matter) thinking about our motives but not feeling them for congruency and truth. Many times our thought and feelings in regard to a specific issue are out of synch. The following examples illustrate three different people in three different situations, displaying three different behaviors. Each believed that their decisions were guided by specific values yet all made decisions motivated by the same hidden desire.

Sam broke up with his girlfriend of three years. She got upset and stopped communicating with him, and Sam understood her need for silence … until the day, they met in public and she ignored him. Sam became obsessed with the idea that they needed to talk. He was persistent with attempts to reconnect with is ex girlfriend, but she refused to talk to him. No longer understanding her attitude, Sam insisted that he *just* wanted her to understand his decision. When asked why it was important that she understood his decision, Sam said "Because she seems hurting and I don't want her to hurt." Motivated by his hidden desire that his ex girlfriend has a good opinion of him, yet unaware of it, Sam truly believed that his motive was concern for her feelings. In some way it was, but most importantly Sam was concerned about her feelings for him. He did not want her to dislike him. After all, it was his decision to break up, it was his desire to explain and understand things, not hers. If Sam's motive was really his concern for her feelings, he would not have pestered her to talk about a painful situation.

Katherine her management position in a large company to start her own consulting business. Priding herself on being someone who helps the underdog, she decided to help some employees get raise they deserved. What Katherine did not realize is that her actions were not motivated to protect the innocent employee as much as there were motivated by a desire to protect her own image. Concerned that people may think that she is ungrateful for leaving the company and a great boss, she unconsciously started undermining the good opinion employees had of her boss. Katherine started suggesting that the boss was unfair, that the employees deserved a raise, and confided information that the employees should not have known. Unaware of her hidden motives, Katherine believed that she was helping the unfortunate. She believed that her actions were motivated by her desire to save few people before leaving the company. Consumed with her idea of helping others, Katherine felt blindsided when the information she entrusted to her co-workers was used against her. Not only did the employees develop animosity against each other, they also developed resentment toward the boss and Katherine. She was disappointed and hurt, feeling betrayed by people who she wanted to help. Unbeknownst to her, Katherine's true motivation was her desire for others to have a good opinion of her. Katherine felt guilty and doubtful that she was leaving a company and the boss she enjoyed, and consequently she felt a need to justify her decision. Unconsciously, she needed to portray her boss as unfair and she needed others to see him in the same light. In order for her to display injustice and assume the role of a protector, Katherine volunteered information about how much some employees were paid, truly believing that her motivation was to help others. Ironically, her actions did not protect them, but made them unhappy and resentful. Because she was unaware of her feelings of guilt and doubt and the way those feelings affected her decisions, Katherine was offended by the entire situation. If she really wanted to help them, she would have taken the time to speak to her boss about the employees, praise their accomplishments and if possible, negotiate a raise for them. If Katherine did not feel guilty about leaving the company, she would have not needed to view her boss as the bad guy, and she could have performed a noble act of quiet negotiation.

Christopher is an owner of a service oriented mid-size company. The business was booming and he was proud of his accomplishments. Six months prior, he dared to position his product on the market at a higher than average price. The customers responded well, and Christopher was happy. Since the business was doing well, he decided to renovate his office. For the first time, he hired a professional decorator. He came from a lower middle class background, and having a decorator projected the image of wealth he had always dreamed about. The renovations were finished and the bill was exorbitant. Christopher was shocked. More than shocked, Christopher was furious. Before the renovations began, he asked the decorator for her hourly rate and thought he could afford it, but he had never anticipated the number of hours she claimed. Christopher knew that the number of hours spent on designing and executing the renovation were exaggerated. Although mad about the situation and sure in his knowledge that the price for the work performed was unreasonably high, Christopher was considering paying the bill. Fearful of running out of money he started contemplating raising prices of his product to cover for the unexpected expense. In his mind, charging his customers was justified with the cost of running the business. Ironically, while Christopher complained that the interior designer overcharged him, he was planning to overcharge his own customers. Instead of *justifying* the change in pricing his product, he should have *questioned* his motives for changing prices. When asked about the reason for paying a bill he knew was exaggerated, he answered "I do not like to argue. I would rather pay the bill and avoid a conflict." In reality, Christopher wanted the designer to think of him as a prosperous person. If he had questioned the bill, she could have thought of him as poor–an image Christopher did not want anyone to have of him. Interestingly, he did not consider that questioning exaggerated bill would make her think of him as a smart person who has money but does not spend it blindly. Unaware of his hidden desire, Christopher's concern with the interior designer's opinion of him almost cost him his business.

Many of us make similar decisions. Unaware of our feelings, we think our actions are guided by one value; meanwhile, we are unconsciously driven by another. We collectively lack awareness about our true motivation; sometimes we wish to know what drive us to repeat certain mistakes and other times we wish to know what could motivate us out of a rut.

The way to develop personal awareness is to pay attention to our thoughts and feelings, our decisions and actions. Thoughts and feelings are two sides of the same coin; both functions assist us in making decisions. Most people believe that the less attention they give their feelings, the better their capacity to think logically and make rational decisions will be. However, just the opposite is true: to think logically and to make effective decisions one has to be able to feel.

Developing personal awareness requires intentional effort. Ideally, personal awareness develops with maturity. From birth to death, we gradually become aware of our uniqueness, our willpower, and our choices. Unfortunately, our personal awareness does not develop in tandem with our age. People rarely become wise spontaneously. To be wise, we have to pay attention and reflect upon our-selves continuously. Personal awareness develops upward, like climbing a spiral staircase. We keep rotating around the same issues of self-discovery, self-expres-sion, and self-actualization; gaining expanded points of view with every step.

Developing personal awareness is beneficial for two reasons: first, to avoid hav-ing double standards and conflicting beliefs, and second, to consciously seek out limited beliefs and standards and transform them. If we develop a habit to exam-ine our motivations and decisions on a regular basis, and take mental notes of things we value as important, then we do not have to wait for incidents such as accidents, divorce, or illness to wake us up and urge us to redefine our priorities.

In the constantly changing world, we have to remain alert. Our awareness is the stage for personal transformation; the larger the stage, the bigger the transfor-mation. Having awareness of self, our uniqueness and how it relates to our deci-sions allows us to live our truth—to experience and express our true power and freedom.

Chapter Fifteen
Emotional Fitness: Three Exercises to Get You in Shape

Emotional intelligence refers to our ability to understand, manage, and appropriately utilize our emotions. Emotional fitness is having the mental agility to apply emotional intelligence. An emotionally intelligent and emotionally fit person can balance between the mind and the heart, between thinking and feeling. When emotion enters our awareness, our mind needs to be open to receive the messenger, available to think about the meaning of the message and possible options, alert to evaluate options on a feeling scale, and skillful to make the most appropriate and congruent decision for a given situation. Consequently, to be emotionally smart we don't need to control our emotions; rather, we need to be *flexible* about them.

Emotional fitness is about developing inner strength and achieving a sense of inner balance and power. The premise of this book is that you are in charge of your life. You can choose your thoughts and feelings and make deliberate decisions. You can benefit from your feelings by intentionally choosing those that transform your inner energy and thereby contribute to your inner peace and growth.

Being in control of a challenging situation depends on the harmony between our intellect and our sentiment. Emotional fitness exercises are designed with the intention of helping you put more thinking into feeling and vice versa. Thinking and feeling are like muscles working together; just as the inner adjustment of our muscles provide us with balance and movement, the fine-tuning of information provided by thinking and feeling gives us balance and strength. Feelings help us to sense, and thinking helps us to understand, the state of our vital energy; both assist us in achieving the state we desire. In fear, we restrict and contain our energy; in faith, we expand it beyond what is visible. If internally paralyzed by fear, we can add faith to regain inner movement. Just as we need both legs to walk with balance and vigor, we need both thinking and feeling to progress in life.

The need for emotional fitness arises when our inner energy is stuck, scattered, or insufficient to tackle the challenges that our lives present. The objective of becoming emotionally fit is to be prepared and capable of transforming our inner energy as needed. Since our inner energy is fluid and malleable, the emotional fitness exercises that follow are not rigid, "how-to" steps; they are comprised of questions intended to guide you through transformation. These questions are designed to elicit a different way of thinking and thereby cause change.

There are three simple exercises that can help you become emotionally fit: Cleaning Your Emotional Closet, Stress Surfing, and Emotion Shopping. These exercises, in turn, correlate to the times in which emotional experiences occur: past, present, and future. If the event that is causing your undesirable feelings already happened, then you can observe it, examine it, and learn from it. You can sort through your feelings and file them away. Whenever you sort through something, you make "keep" and "toss" piles, and then you prioritize your "keep" pile. You can do the same thing with feelings from the past. You first decide which feelings to toss and which to keep, and then you file the retained feelings according to their purpose. Remember, emotions can teach you about who you are, give you the opportunity to express your uniqueness, and help you stretch to your potential. For example, anger can teach you about your boundaries, help you delineate your limits and demonstrate them for others, or fuel your determination and help you accomplish a goal.

If your experience is happening here and now, then your focus is on synchronizing thinking and feeling and on managing your inner energy. The ability to manage emotions in-the-moment requires you to prioritize your actions and adjust your attitude in the midst of a stressful situation. Imagine being told on Tuesday that if you do not meet your sales quota by Friday your job will be terminated. You panic. Your mind off track, worrying about Friday, you're incapable of thinking straight. Identifying your intention to work with passion and integrity, you recognize that worrying about Friday ahead of time is unproductive. You elicit a feeling of confidence by remembering your resourcefulness. You change your attitude from panic to resolution, and you concentrate on making phone calls. Your focus is on working miracles, and you expect to make the sales needed to meet the required quota. You create an inner challenge, fill yourself with curiosity and determination, and shift your mental mode from "overloaded" to "sharp."

Finally, if the event causing you distress has yet to happen, you can use these exercises to set the tone and direction for your future experience. If you are afraid to make a move in life because you don't know what may happen, you can think about faith until the feelings of confidence and trust are generated strongly enough to counteract your fear. You can also envision results beyond fear and focus on that vision to build courage and transcend dread. Or like me, you can choose to experience fear in a fun setting to remind you that fear does not always have to come with pain. When I feel paralyzed by fear, I choose some fun activity in which I can face my fear, yet laugh, such as going on a scary ride in a water park or flying on a trapeze.

Before we proceed with the exercises, let's explore two important factors in achieving emotional empowerment: honesty and intention. As the saying goes, the truth will set you free. Being honest with yourself will free up your energy from getting stuck in the ruts of "pretend" and "should be." The more you pretend to be who you think you should be, the less you will feel your energy to be free and flowing. There is an interesting phenomenon in our society. We are obsessed with the idea of not hurting anyone's feelings. Unfortunately, this originally benevolent intention has become distorted. Under the guise of protecting other people's feelings, we got sidetracked into pretending and being dishonest.

An innocent, yet prevalent, problem people have is being "too nice." There is a difference between helping, serving, and pleasing others. In helping, you feel energized. In serving, you feel proud of your accomplishment. In pleasing, you feel consumed and resentful. Pleasing is different from deciding to do something that gives you pleasure. When we are focused on pleasing others at the expense of ourselves, we are acting against our will, and thereby communicating a lie. We please others to prevent hurting their feelings or to avoid their discontentment and dislike. One way to look at our need to please someone is to see it as an indication that we are insecure about our worth and that we think we should be nice and pleasing in order to get love and acceptance from others. If you are focused solely on pleasing others, you are disrespecting and—therefore being dishonest with—both yourself and others. You wouldn't want others to lie to you, so what makes you believe that others want you to fake your willingness to serve?

The other side of our need to please is our difficulty in saying no. If you are one of those people who have difficulty saying no to others, think about this: If you ask me to do you a favor and I look into your eyes and tell you with sincerity, "I would really love to help you but I am tired," would you stop liking me because of my honesty? Probably not. You may be briefly disappointed, but most likely, you would understand. Pleasing violates our nature. Dishonesty may avoid short-term disturbance, but it creates long-term tensions, while honesty replaces short-term discomfort for long-term harmony. You can be considerate of other people, take into account their point-of-view, and be gentle in your approach, but keep in mind that the greatest gift you can give to someone is truthfulness.

The second factor in achieving emotional empowerment is intention. Emotions are messengers informing you about the way you engage in life. The messages emotions relate to you provide valuable information about a specific situation. They show you if your decisions and values are congruent by making you feel a certain way. Emotions also give you the opportunity to evaluate your position and adjust your action or attitude. Intention is the spin, or direction and movement, you give to your inner energy. Intention is like a pointer showing the final destination of your decision. Beware of your intention because it will determine your overall feeling.

If your intention and actions are out of synch, you will feel emotional discomfort. For example, after making a mistake you feel disappointed and scared. Although the event is over, your brooding and self-criticism over the mistake causes you emotional pain. Your intention is not to repeat the mistake, but your self-criticism is triggering the opposite effect. Instead of building your self-esteem and helping you feel more secure the next time you approach a similar situation, you feel insecure and doubtful. Your action is counterproductive to your intention.

Furthermore, if your values are to support and encourage others, then beating yourself up over a mistake is incongruent with those values. Once you realize that your self-criticism is detrimental to your intention to improve, you can change your attitude. With your disappointment replaced with confidence, and your energy shifted, you will automatically file that memory of the event into the past and become free to move on.

Always be mindful of your intention! What do you want to accomplish in a given situation? Do you want to impress, hurt, blame others, or explain yourself? Do you want to express and demonstrate your true uniqueness or take charge and responsibility for your life? Are your thoughts and actions aligned with your intention? Is your intention aligned with your values? Question yourself as often as possible—not to cause doubt, but to find truth and inner harmony.

The following three exercises are guidelines to help you develop a new way of thinking—one that is built around your feelings:

1. **Cleaning Your Emotional Closet** is an exercise that enables you to look into your past experiences and sort through them. This exercise gives you time to practice emotional fitness at your leisure. Similar to the way you look through your clothes while cleaning your closet, deciding which clothes to keep and which to throw away, this exercise guides you to do the same with your past emotional experiences. You try them on to determine their comfort and function; some experiences you keep, others you discard, and for those that are significant but unpleasant, you redefine their meaning and purpose.

   The objective of this exercise is to help you better understand the circumstances of, your perception of, and your involvement in a given situation so that you can learn something beneficial from it and then file the memory of the event "out of your mind." Practicing this exercise will prepare you for the next two exercises, Stress Surfing and Emotion Shopping.

   Before you proceed, let me again emphasize the importance of writing down your answers. Writing forces you to separate your feelings. When thinking about an emotionally charged situation, your emotions overlap; but when you are writing about them, finding the correct word to describe your feeling forces you to address your emotions one at the time.

   Start cleaning your emotional closet by following the steps below. Write down your answers and observations.

   a. Select a situation that bothered you and list at least five feelings associated with it. (Refer to table 2 of the "Tables" section.)

      1_____

      2_____

      3_____

      4_____

      5_____

   b. What is the message of each individual feeling? Write it down. (Refer to table 3 of the "Tables" section.)

      1_____

      _____

2 _____

_____

3 _____

_____

4 _____

_____

5 _____

_____

c. What is the meaning you assigned to the situation? If the same situation happened to someone else, would you assign the same meaning to it? Depersonalize your experience. Look at the setting required for the emotion to occur, and from that point of view examine your position in it objectively.

_____
_____
_____
_____
_____
_____
_____
_____
_____

d. Emotions are shaped by our perception. How did you perceive yourself in the situation? Was your heart open or closed? Were you offensive, defensive, or neutral? Did you view yourself as a victim or as a contender? (Refer to table 3 of the "Tables" section.)

_____
_____
_____
_____
_____
_____
_____
_____
_____

e.   What was your intention? How did you perceive others involved in this situation and what did you believe was their intention? Examine the intentions of all parties, including yourself.

_____
_____
_____
_____
_____
_____
_____
_____
_____

f.   Did you accomplish what you really wanted in this situation? If not, what did you accomplish?

_____
_____
_____
_____
_____
_____
_____
_____

g.   If you had the opportunity to engage in the same situation again, would you view it the same way, act the same way, feel the same way? If not, what would you feel instead? Write down the meanings and feelings you would prefer to associate to this situation.

_____
_____
_____
_____
_____
_____
_____
_____

h. Go back to your original list. From the five feelings listed above, identify the strongest feeling. What was the purpose of this messenger? To teach you about your value, to give you the opportunity to communicate your standards or to express your uniqueness? Decide how you want to "file" the experience. Do you want to keep it and for what reason, or do you want to discard it?

_____
_____
_____
_____
_____
_____
_____
_____
_____
_____

2. **Stress Surfing** is an exercise to help you manage your emotions on the spot. Since you don't have much time at your disposal, you have to be quick on your feet. To surf through a stressful situation, you need mental agility to switch back and forth from thinking to sensing. Like in windsurfing, you must know your intention in order to adjust your sail (your perception) and regulate the wind in your sail (your attitude) in order to reach your desired destination (your desired result).

    The objective of this exercise is to become aware of the relationship between your thoughts and feelings and the ways they influence your energy. When you learn to identify and intentionally elicit thoughts and feelings that can move you in the desired direction, you achieve emotional mastery.

    a. **Determine the wind.** In order to sail, you need to be aware of the wind. In stress surfing, you need to be aware of your inner energy. If, at any given time you are not "sailing" in a desired direction, allow yourself to identify what feeling is distracting you. Identify the strongest feeling and decipher its message. For example, stress is about considering too many things with equal importance. Feeling overwhelmed results from looking at too large of a picture. Irritation results from giving too much attention to detail. Frustration is about having an overly narrow or strict vision concerning your approach or expectation. (For more information, refer to tables 1 and 3 of the "Tables" section.)

        _____

        _____

        _____

        _____

        _____

        _____

        _____

        _____

        _____

    b. **Evaluate your position in the wind.** Consider your present position. Evaluate the conditions eliciting your current state, and examine what to change in order to transform your position. Remember, you cannot change the wind, but you can change the position of your sail. What are you thinking? What are you sensing? What is happening with your energy? Turn your attention inward, and pay attention to its movement and sensation of energy. Where is your energy taking you? Now, change your point of view. Notice your feelings. Change the meaning attached to the situation. Notice your feelings.

_____

_____

_____

_____

_____

_____

_____

_____

_____

c.   **Adjust the sail.** Decide your direction and destination. What is your intention? What is your desired feeling or outcome? What action or attitude would take you to your final destination? What do you want to accomplish? Select thoughts that can generate your desired feeling. What really matters in this situation? Evaluate your strongest feeling, and focus on it. (Refer to table 2 of the "Tables" section.)

_____

_____

_____

_____

_____

_____

_____

_____

_____

Shifting to a neutral position. Sometimes a particular emotional wind may be too strong for us to redirect our sails. In that type of situation, instead of resisting the wind and holding on to the stress, letting the storm pass by is a wise decision. Too many messengers at a time can cause mental overload and incapacitate our brain to think clearly. Acknowledge that you cannot think clearly at the moment and your best course of action to avoid further miscommunication might be to do nothing. For example, when you recognize that you are in the midst of a heated argument, follow these steps:

    a.   As you recognize the emotional storm, call for a time-out. **State your immediate intention.** For example, say that your intention is not to offend the other person or dismiss his point of view but that in this specific moment you are not in a frame of mind to think clearly, and you need time to gain clarity. Taking the time to compose yourself, instead of reacting to the situation, shows respect to everyone involved. By doing so, you demonstrate to the other party that you are aware of your emotional state and in charge of it, and the act itself is empowering.

       For practice, recall a situation in which you could have benefited from taking a time out and shifting your stressful feelings to neutral. Write down your immediate intention here.

_____

_____

_____

    b.   Focus on evoking a feeling of peace and calm within yourself. Detach from the perception and meaning that generated the emotional flood. Imagine having a mute button to quiet everything around you for thirty seconds. Become an observer. **Clear your mind.** Describe a scene, such as a beautiful sunset or the face of your dog, which can quickly evoke a feeling of peace and calm.

_____

_____

_____

c. **Recommit to your intention for the situation.** Resume stress surfing and follow the steps explained above: determine the wind, evaluate your position, and adjust the sail. Write down the intention you have for the situation. What do you want to accomplish?

_____

_____

_____

3. **Emotion Shopping** is an exercise about attending to your needs and desires. If you had no needs or desires, you would stop evolving. When you go shopping, you envision what you would like to get, and then you search for the item. Emotion shopping works the same way. In emotion shopping, you envision where you want to be with regard to your energy, and you look for the thoughts and feelings that can take you there. For example, you want to feel comfortable and confident speaking in public. You imagine what it feels like to be confident. Then you find a situation with a similar setting that could generate desired feelings, such as being at a dinner with a group of friends and talking about a subject that is your passion. In that situation, you would be talking to a group of people, feeling relaxed and confident. Then as you start preparing for speaking in public, you keep your image of dinner in mind and a feeling of confidence in your spirit. As you progress with speaking, you eventually feel so comfortable that you no longer need the imaginative foreplay. The objective of this exercise is to determine the direction and destination for your future attitude; identify feelings you want to feel at you final destination, choose thoughts that can take you there, and keep your focus on the destination.

   a. **Establish your starting place.** Where do you stand emotionally in relation to your goal? List at least three feelings that describe your present state or the attitude you want to change. What keeps you there? What stands in your way? List as many reasons as possible in order to discover your self-limiting beliefs and feelings. What are your thoughts or beliefs that generate undesired feelings?

      _____
      _____
      _____
      _____
      _____
      _____
      _____
      _____

   b. **Examine your possible destinations.** What would you rather feel or believe? List at least three feelings that describe your desired attitude. What do you want to accomplish? Is what you desire going to expand or stabilize your energy? Is your desire aligned with your values? Examine what motivates you. Look for the situations that make you feel more alive; they are the fuel pumps for your uniqueness and they will make the transformation effortless. Write down at least two things that could motive you to change.

_____
_____
_____
_____
_____
_____
_____
_____

c. **Envision what would happen if you *do not* change.** What is the worst thing that could happen to you if you stay in the same place or continue to feel the old way? How would you feel if that happens? List at least three feelings. If the worst thing does take place, then what happens after? What do you think are the consequences? Are the consequences fatal or temporary?

_____
_____
_____
_____
_____
_____
_____
_____

d. **Envision what would happen if you *do* change.** Is your goal congruent with your values and your uniqueness? Imagine yourself as already having reached your destination. Imagine you have already experienced the new feeling. What additional feelings do you have? List at least three feelings. Having achieved this goal, what happens next? Expand your vision and taste your future. Does it fit you?

_____
_____

_____
_____
_____
_____
_____
_____
_____

e.   **Focus on your destination.** Choose the lead feeling and keep your attention on it. Focus on the energy, its direction, and its intensity. Identify thoughts and feelings that can take you in the desired direction, and then focus on them. Write down the behavior you would display if you actually felt the way you want to feel. Maintain an image in your mind that elicits the desired feeling. Bring up the desired feeling, adjust your attitude, and internally hold on to it.

_____
_____
_____
_____
_____
_____
_____
_____

The objective of becoming emotionally fit is to be prepared and capable of transforming our inner energy as needed. Life is constantly changing, our personalities consistently evolving; therefore, the way we deal with life has to be flexible too. The exercises suggested above are like recipes; they provide a list of suggested ingredients, but it's up to you to mix and match them to suit your unique taste. Question your perception, values, and the meaning you assign to events, constantly sensing your energy. Remember to always keep in mind the type of dish you're making; never lose sight of your intention.

Chapter Sixteen
Beware of the Ego

My friend Patricia was in a challenging marriage. She frequently complained that her husband treated her as if she were ignorant, talking down to her and behaving as if her feelings and opinions did not matter. One evening Patricia and her husband invited me to their house for dinner, where I witnessed their interaction.

While they were preparing dinner, Patricia acted distracted. Her husband, Denis, proposed to cook dinner by himself, offering Patricia and me time to chat. Patricia insisted on participating in the dinner preparation. However, Patricia would start doing something and then lose sight of her task, mindlessly stand in the middle of the kitchen, or abandon her task, distracted by something brought up in our conversation. On a few occasions, Denis reminded her of her task and the option of letting him finish the dinner by himself. His voice was calm, and his requests were patient. After a certain number of seemingly unheard suggestions, he turned to me—half apologetic, half protective—and said that Patricia was going through menopause and had difficulty dealing with hormonal changes.

As the evening progressed, Patricia's state didn't improve, and Denis's voice became a little irritated. Patricia was defensive and snappy. Aware of his own irritation, Denis shared with me that Patricia's behavior had changed in the last few months and resulted, once again, from her menopausal hormonal troubles. He never yelled at her, but we could sense his frustration. Interestingly, the "relaxing" evening of cooking together had turned into a stressful event. The tension between them subsided as we finished dinner. Although we enjoyed our food, time, and conversation, the evening's events revealed the underlying stressful dynamic between my friends.

A few days later I met with Patricia for lunch. Wanting to help her, I brought up the evening and shared my perspective with her. I hoped to show Patricia another side of her relationship and help her see that Denis really loved her and cared for her feelings. But Patricia wasn't hearing me. Her mind was locked into perceiving him as a verbal tyrant. I mentioned that she had been behaving strangely that evening and that his frustration was understandable.

Patricia could not see Denis's point of view. She was stuck in her point of view that he was a mental tyrant. I tried to have her take her husband's position and asked her how she would feel if he were behaving mindlessly. My explanation didn't reach her. Patricia objected: "But you don't hear the undertone in his voice. He speaks to me like a child. He tells me what to do." My reply to her was that he had to tell her what to do because she was not helping him. In my opinion, he was not arguing her lack of intelligence but expressing his frustration because he knew she was smart but did not act accordingly. He was annoyed that he had to tell her what to do.

Needless to say, Patricia was not willing to give up her defensive point of view. Since she could not blame Denis anymore, she started making excuses for her behavior; she had a headache, didn't sleep sufficiently, and began to demonstrate other signs that she was not willing to change her point-of-view. Patricia had an image of herself to protect, and she was focusing hard on her task. She was trying to show me that she was smart. She was concerned that her behavior could tarnish her reputation, affect my perception of her, and cause me to stop loving her.

I explained to Patricia that neither her husband nor I ever questioned her intelligence. We both loved her because of her personality, not because she's "perfectly intelligent." I told her that, instead of being offended by Denis's frustration, she could have noticed it as a messenger and discovered its cause. Acknowledging her state of mind as an inconvenience to both of them, she could have asked her husband to be patient with her. If she had accepted her behavior as a temporary state, and was not concerned about our opinion of her intelligence, she could have used the opportunity to build a stronger partnership with her husband instead of opposition.

Although my suggestion appealed to her, Patricia's ego was kicking and screaming, still not ready to give in. Because making excuses for her behavior was no longer logical, she was now looking to explain her defensive behavior. "You don't know how he talks to me at home. He was polite because you were there." I love Patricia and really care for her, so I continued to challenge her. My intention was to show her that she was the only person holding onto this image of how she should be in order for us to love and respect her.

Patricia's image of herself was a meaningless expectation fabricated in her mind, making her unhappy with herself. Because of her "should be" image, she was projecting rejection onto herself without any external influence. I told her that I thought she was already perfect—even during the days when she's goofy—and we both laughed. I told her that perfection is having all of the colors in the spectrum, and because of her colorful personality, we love her dearly.

Finally, Patricia let go of her defenses. We hugged and shared how much we appreciated each other and our friendship. Patricia was energetically drained. She looked at me and said: "This emotion thing you do is not easy stuff."

It was not the "emotion thing" but fighting to keep up with phony images of herself that was exhausting Patricia. "Honesty is effortless," was my reply. A Chinese proverb says, "Tension is who you think you should be. Relaxation is who you are."

There are words we use habitually without really understanding their meaning. *Ego* is one of those words. *Webster's Universal College* dictionary tells us that ego is a thinking, feeling, and conscious being, able to distinguish itself from others. In other words, ego represents self-image, an image we have of our individuality relative to others. If we look at the *American Heritage dictionary,* we would find two definitions for the meaning of ego that somewhat contradict each other. One states that ego is "appropriate pride in oneself; i.e., self-esteem," and the second states that ego is "an exaggerated sense of self-importance." But, how do we know whether our image of self is appropriate or exaggerated?

Before we answer this question, let us explain how we form ego image. Just as the eye needs a mirror to see itself, *I* need others in order to see myself. Others tell us what they like or dislike about us, and they inform us whether we are in agreement with their likes and dislikes. As a result, it is from others that we get the idea of who we are. That *idea* is ego.

A child is born with inactive software called consciousness. As the child interacts with the environment, parts of his consciousness activate, and the child develops an image of society and of himself. For example, we learn to behave in a civilized manner and that education leads to providing for comfortable living. As we accept the rules of society, we also feel accepted.

At our early stage of existence we are not self-sufficient; consequently, we need others to care for us. Because of our dependence on others for survival, we inherently fear rejection. For that reason, every human being has some degree of fear of rejection. As we mature, we are meant to understand our fear and evaluate it appropriately. Infantile fear is justifiable because an infant's survival depends on everyone else's acceptance. An adult obsessed with acceptance is infantile; a mature individual should be discriminatory about whose acceptance and approval is relevant.

In the process of our social development, our ego's image helps us evolve and integrate in society. To protect us and help us "survive" in the world around us, our parents project the image of what we should do and should be as guidelines for our development. These guidelines protect us in the same way that street signs protect us when we drive. Imagine if there were no roads and no signs; we would all kill each other driving aimlessly. Society sets values and rules for us to follow so that our lives will have structure and comfort. The images and conclusions we make about ourselves and our environment help us interact easier. For example, there is an existing image of the appropriate dress code associated with business, exercise, or mountain climbing and most of us dress according to the "dress code image." Similarly, we have an idea, an image of appropriate and acceptable behaviors that are specific to social settings, such as being smart in school and gregarious at a party, and we behave according to that image.

As we learn society's rules of engagement, we also misinterpret them as judgments. We form the idea that we have to be a certain way to assure our place in society and thereby our survival. Because we fear social rejection, sometimes our behavior is senseless and counterproductive to our true desires. Men who believe they should not cry yet desire consolation, may grieve silently, feeling lonely and isolated, incapable of expressing their true feelings.

The image of self we form as children is "what we should be" but as adults, we have the responsibility to harmonize this image with "what we could be." If we fail this responsibility, we risk creating inner conflict and an exaggerated fear of rejection.

The following example illustrates how my images of myself created conflicting values, thus inner tension. When I was a child, having good grades was very important to the adults around me, so I formed the belief that being smart was a requirement to my social acceptance. I also learned that education was the path to a better life. Cultivating my intelligence and investing in my education became the theme of my life. Although my intelligence helped me reach a desired lifestyle, it also caused me a lot of social anxiety and emotional suffering. As a young adult, I spent years proving my intelligence to everyone I encountered. Motivated by survival and driven by the fear of rejection, I obsessed over maintaining an image of myself as a smart person. Although my intention to show superior intelligence was to get closer to others, my behavior drove people away. Discovering this inner discrepancy helped me achieve peace within.

The purpose of ego is to give us an internal guideline to support us in quickly assessing our position in the world. To respond appropriately to the purpose of ego, we need to learn to use its image to evaluate—rather than to judge—ourselves. When we judge our position instead of evaluating it, we focus on rejection instead of integration and we have the tendency to determine something or someone as good or bad, superior or inferior, or special vs. ordinary. When we judge ourselves instead of evaluating, we enter the gray area of ego by crossing from the "appropriate pride in oneself; i.e., self-esteem," to "an exaggerated sense of self-importance."

Beware of ego. The information we receive from the ego should serve as a gauge for our social integration, not as a way to exclude ourselves from others. Understanding how ego relates to our thinking and feeling is subtle, and for that reason, I will use another example from my life to illustrate when the ego gets in our way.

I grew up in the lower middle class. We didn't have much money or many expensive things, but we never missed a meal, lacked clothing, or passed up an opportunity to laugh. When I started going to school, I heard other children talk about the importance of what they had, and their judgment put a dent in my image of my life. Before the comparison, I was happy with my life situation; after the comparison, I suffered. It wasn't the conditions that bothered me, but the fact that they could cause rejection from my peers.

The purpose of the ego image is to provide feedback so we can adjust our behavior and *synchronize* our individuality with others; however, we often misinterpret this purpose. The ego image is supposed to unify us with others—not divide us. In Patricia's example, her image of a "perfect self" was making her perceive Denis' comments as attacks to her personality, which promoted her defensiveness. Instead of hearing her husband's comments as supportive, she was interpreting them as a criticism. Had the comments been coming from a stranger, Patricia would not have had an image to protect, and so, would not feel defensive. Instead of using the given opportunity to deepen her relationship, Patricia was creating distance in it. Patricia's source of self-disapproval was her image—not Denis' comments.

We would be wise to use the ego to evaluate our lives and improve them, not to destroy them. In that regard, whenever we notice that the image we have created about ourselves is promoting self-disapproval, it is our responsibility to update our mental software from what we "should be" to what we "could be."

Feelings are messengers. Whenever you feel internally divided, you are being given the opportunity to reevaluate your self-image. The more aware you are of your uniqueness and the way it relates to society, the easier it is for you to tweak your image so it more accurately expresses your truth. Whether it is relating to others or to ourselves, we should always experience inner harmony.

PART FIVE
Personal Stories

The happiest people don't necessarily have the best of everything; they just make the best of everything that comes along their way.

Anonymous

Emotional matters are personal and often kept secret. Because we are not emotionally educated most of us don't understand our own feelings, so it's no wonder we find it difficult to interpret the feelings of others. I simply don't have the same degree of access to your thoughts and feelings as I do to my own. My beliefs and convictions about emotions derive from my own experiences of transformation. The first reason for selecting personal stories to share with you is to give you an insight into my thinking and feeling.

Another reason I have selected to share my personal stories is to encourage you to welcome your feelings and accept their messages without judgment. People have the tendency to judge feelings instead of evaluating their messages. Some of my stories may sound irrelevant, or my feelings may seem exaggerated. The feelings described in this section were my reality, whether they make sense to you or not. Similarly, your feelings are your reality. Do not worry if they don't make sense to others. Feelings are your *personal* messengers, and you are meant to accept them and heed their messages. By being impartial toward your emotions you will free yourself from judgment and inner struggle.

Each of the stories I am about to share with you utilizes the emotional fitness exercises outlined in the previous section. As we have discovered, transforming feelings happens by applying various exercises as needed. As you read the personal accounts that follow, try to identify the specific steps that led to transformation:

    a.   Clarifying feelings by expanding emotional vocabulary

    b.   Identifying the main emotion messenger

    c.   Deciphering the message

    d.   Identifying perspective

    e.   Creating transformation

My intention for this section is to use my personal stories to demonstrate how emotional intelligence and emotional fitness can be applied. I hope that by walking with me through my life experiences and witnessing my process of emotional transformation you will find the courage and motivation to set upon your own path of change.

Chapter Seventeen
I'm Sorry You Feel That Way

✦

(Anger)

My plane landed at noon on Friday, my car was ready for pick up from the repair shop, and I had plenty of time to finish my errands before meeting friends for dinner. My plan seemed easy to accomplish until the delay at the car repair shop. After two hours of waiting I was informed that the keys to my car were lost and could not be replaced until Monday. They offered me a complimentary rental car. The solution would have been perfect if I didn't have to leave town early Sunday. The rental car was due back on Monday. I was upset because of the waiting and additional complications to my tight schedule posed by the rental car return, but I decided to keep my cool, anyway. After all, I was the emotion expert.

The clerk pointed me to the rental counter where I had to wait in line for another twenty minutes. As I was standing in line my patience was slowly eroded by feelings of injustice and anger. Keeping my composure, listening to my emotional messengers, and processing their messages, my decision was to focus on signing the rental agreement and getting out of there as quickly as possible.

Communicating with an expressionless car-rental clerk was not the most pleasant experience, but I decided not to care. I had a plan, and I was determined not to let the situation spoil my day. The rental car was on its way. I was soon to be free.

After patiently waiting for another fifteen minutes for someone to bring me the car I went searching for the clerk. Yes, searching, because he was nowhere to be found. He had forgotten about me and was enjoying his break. Should I say that my list of emotions waiting to be processed was getting longer with every minute spent there? I felt neglected, disrespected, rejected, frustrated, disappointed, and sad, but mostly, I was angry.

My list of unpleasant emotions grew longer as the unhappy clerk finally pulled up in a car with a flat tire. I complained, which made us both more aggravated. He brought another car and wanted me to drive it away without any notation of our heated exchange. I expressed my concern and he dismissed it. I asked for his name, and he gave it to me reluctantly, further irritating both of us. Steaming, I finally drove away.

Two blocks down the road a light on the dashboard caught my attention. The gas tank was empty. Did I mention I was angry? More precisely, I was furious. Needless to say, my emotion-expert hat was off, and I was on my way to share a piece of my mind with the clerk.

In a respectful yet angry voice I told him that the way he handled my situation was inappropriate and inconsiderate and that I was very disappointed and angry. "I'm sorry that you feel that way," he responded in a bored, emotionless voice. He proceeded to say that he didn't see any reason to be upset because the rental agreement stated that the car should be returned with the gas tank filled to the same level as when it was received. Then he walked away to resume his break, wishing me a nice evening.

Totally in shock and reeling from the turmoil of my emotions, I sat in the car and drove away. My entire body was shaking. Aware of my distress, I pulled over and called upon my reason to help me out. My emotional messengers were too rowdy, and I desperately needed my clear thinking to get involved again. As my thinking capacity returned, I addressed one emotion at a time. My anger was telling me that the way my situation was handled violated my standards of customer service, respect, and care for another person's time and feelings. Feeling angry was the opportunity to express my values, and I did share them with the clerk. I was proud of the way I handled my part of the situation. My anger subsided but did not disappear.

I explored my other feelings of neglect and disrespect. Although my feelings were appropriate, their intensity was overwhelming, showing me that I had attached too much importance to the situation. Wasting one afternoon and having my list of errands unchecked was not the end of the world. Having the clerk—an irrelevant person in my life—show me lack of attention and respect should not matter *that* much. Looking at my situation again and measuring its importance against my personal significance scale deflated my feelings of neglect and disrespect.

Then the feeling of anger surfaced again. As I started thinking about the clerk, my stomach started churning, and the noise in my head growled. I was getting upset again, heading in the direction of having my evening destroyed as well.

This was not the direction I had planned for my day. I thought about the insignificance of the situation and the opportunity I had to express my values. Once again, I had to choose my attitude. To think about the clerk would waste my energy and make him more important than me. After all, I was insignificant in his life, and he demonstrated that. He didn't care about me and my situation; why should I waste my thoughts on him?

So I shifted my attention. I started thinking of my friends, and, looking forward to telling them about my day, determined to focus on the way I handled the situation rather than the clerk. I chose to view the experience as a major test of my emotional fitness, and I passed it. I decided to focus on pride instead of anger, and I smiled. I will not lie to you. It took me several weeks before I felt totally at ease with what happened that day. I realized that whenever I would ruminate about the event, I had a bad aftertaste. Since I would not serve myself with food that doesn't taste good again and again, I would consciously stop rehashing the situation that gives me unpleasant feelings. Slowly, the emotional memory of the event faded.

The story is ordinary, but its point is not. The intensity of my anger was disproportional to the significance of the event. The intensity of my emotions showed that I was reacting to more than one clerk's behavior. The insignificance of the event helped me distance myself and analyze my feelings. I discovered that the intensity of my feelings was proportional to the sum of all situations in which I had ever felt disrespected. This series of events and the emotions it triggered taught me to address my feelings as they arise and not let them accumulate.

Chapter Eighteen
Teaching Aesthetics

✦

(Frustration)

In addition to being a life coach, I'm also experienced in surgical hair restoration—that is, hair transplantation. At one point in my hair restoration career, I was training a new staff member. Mr. T was to assume the patient coordinator position, and my task was to train him in every aspect of hair restoration. Because of the need to provide a liaison between the non-surgical and the surgical part of hair restoration, and especially to provide patient education, the company expected Mr. T to comprehend every step of the hair restoration process.

Like any other cosmetic surgery, successful hair restoration depends upon the aesthetic awareness of its practitioners. The critical part of hair restoration is recreating natural-looking hairlines. There are certain rules of aesthetics to follow when positioning and shaping a hairline. In the initial consultation, the consultant outlines the future hairline, and during the surgical procedure, the physician makes tiny incisions and creates that hairline. Both persons interacting with the patient have to have a consistent aesthetic view. Mr. T had difficulty comprehending the hairline design.

We started by revisiting the materials provided in the training course. We drew pictures, talked about the rules for an aesthetic design, and seemingly understood each other. However, when the next opportunity presented itself, Mr. T's work demonstrated no improvement.

Although the patients never suffered from M. T's lack of aesthetic sensibilities, I was annoyed because his work required my constant attention. Pulled in too many directions, I felt stressed and irritable. I also felt dismissed and betrayed because I believed his competency when he acquiesced with a sign of understanding. According to my expectations, Mr. T had received enough training to master hairline design. Apparently, however, he did not. Deciding not to be too harsh and giving him the benefit of the doubt, I re-evaluated my approach and came up with a new idea. I located a Styrofoam head and designed the hairline, outlining the rules for the design in different colors. I explained that the rules are important but that the aesthetic judgment is paramount because each face is different. We talked about the importance of a well-designed hairline and discussed the impact of a poorly designed hairline; it could result in a misleading promise or lost business. After we spent a lot of time talking, Mr. T assured me that he understood and had mastered the subject. Our company took pride in the quality of the work delivered, and I was eager to see my pupil succeed.

Proud and satisfied with my approach, I was looking forward to the next opportunity to test Mr. T's knowledge. During the pre-surgical patient consultation, Mr. T was still struggling. No harm was done to the patient and the surgery went well; however, I was not doing well. Frustrated and disappointed, my emotions were in turmoil. Frustrated by my seeming inability to communicate, I was disappointed because Mr. T didn't meet my expectations. I considered him an intelligent person and was bewildered by his inability to accomplish the task. He demonstrated a willingness to learn when asked, and I didn't know what to think about it. From my perspective, he was either dishonest because he confirmed mastering the subject, or he was negligent toward his responsibility. I also took the situation more personally because I saw Mr. T as inconsiderate of my workload and not helping me to alleviate it. For days my frustration and disappointment were flavored with anger. The disappointment was directed toward him and my frustration toward me. My emotional state was disturbing and destructive.

My perception was that he was intentionally doing something to annoy me. I examined my point of view, wondering why Mr. T would do anything to harm me. It didn't make sense that he would do something to sabotage his own progress; he was eager to learn, always respectful, polite, and willing to help. What was preventing both of us from feeling good about the situation?

Then I saw it. Mr. T didn't have an eye for aesthetics. In his mid forties, he was still sporting a Donald Duck neck tie! His idea of aesthetics differed from mine, which explained why he couldn't "get it" and also why I was frustrated. I expected something that was so natural and obvious to me to be the same for him. I assumed that we are all equally aesthetically skilled. Mr. T didn't have the capacity to envision what "aesthetically pleasing" meant in terms of company standards. Once we identified the problem, we were able to find a solution that worked well for everybody involved. Both Mr. T and I felt relieved and satisfied.

We all have encountered situations where things did not go as hoped and people did not behave as expected. My story tells about one of those situations. The significance of my story is my discovering the source of my frustration. First, I assumed that everyone has aesthetic skills. Second, I presumed that Mr. T was intentionally not cooperating. Neither perception was correct or productive. Oftentimes, feelings of frustration bring us the message that it's time to change our expectation or our approach. The example of Mr. T demonstrates that by changing my perception of his skill, I changed my expectation and found a better approach.

Frustration is a messenger that can help you discover your expectations. Even at times when we think we do not have specific expectations, we do. For example, let's say you asked someone to perform a task for you. You desire the task to be finished quickly and you unconsciously set an expectation for the task to be performed within a day or two. Then, as you express your request, you also say politely "take your time," unaware that you are expressing an expectation that is not congruent with your desire. Days pass by and you start feeling frustration because the person is not performing the task at the speed of your unconscious expectation, taking too long to fulfill your request. In this situation, the feeling of frustration can help you uncover the incongruence between your thoughts and actions. Only then you have any hope of creating a better outcome.

This is why you must always be mindful of your expectations. When misunderstandings arise, ask yourself if you were clear about your expectations, and whether you communicated them clearly to others.

Chapter Nineteen
My Father's Abandonment

✦

(Forgiveness)

My father left home while my mother was in the hospital and never returned. A few weeks prior to her surgery, my mother was diagnosed with breast cancer; then her breast was removed and her husband left her with five children. Everything happened so quickly. I could only imagine what she was going through at the time, but somehow my father's disappearance seemed uneventful. He wasn't really involved with our lives. There may be more to the story about my father, but I don't remember much.

I don't recall my father playing with me or my siblings, so his departure didn't affect us as much as it did my mother. I do remember that when he left, I concluded that it was not because of me but due to something between my parents. I kept my focus on my mother, and life slipped back into seeming routine.

In the first year after his departure, my mother would frequently make comments about my father, speculating that he had probably left us because of another woman. I didn't make much of these comments; they did not relate to me. Our lives continued. We occasionally remembered our father—not because we missed him, but because my mother would make comments about his absence.

Four years after my father's departure, my mother died. I was fourteen. I remember the funeral, returning home with my siblings and relatives, and realizing that I would never see my mother again. I don't know what prompted me to believe that my father would come back—maybe a childish desire to believe in impossible dreams. Or, maybe I was scared and wanted him to come home and alleviate my fears. Oddly, on the day of the funeral my father's cousin came to assist with the burial, but my father never showed up.

I remember the evening after the funeral vividly. Everyone was gone, leaving me alone to feel the sadness of my mother's departure and the gnawing fear of an uncertain future. It was long past my bedtime; I couldn't wait for my father any longer. For the first time, I felt that my father didn't care about me or about our family. He had chosen something or someone else as more important than living with his children. This time my father's absence felt like abandonment, probably because my mother wasn't there. The disappointment of knowing that he didn't love or care for me was painful. I knew my mother was gone forever, but what should I do about my father?

I was a strong-willed fourteen-year-old girl. I remember thinking that if my father could decide not to care, so could I. I walked through my bedroom door leaving any hope of having a caring father behind. As I closed the bedroom door, so I closed my heart. Life continued, and nobody ever talked about my father again.

Many years later, while re-examining my painful childhood experiences, I realized how much resentment I had against my father. I became hostile and angry just thinking of him. He abandoned us in a very cruel manner—when my mother and I needed him the most. The wrong done to us was unfair. I was tight inside, filled with resentment but incapable of letting go. I was trapped between the desire to forgive and the inability to do so. I wanted to free myself from the unpleasant bitterness that the abandonment left with me, but I was trapped by my own attachment.

Even though I made a conscious decision to forgive, the act of forgiveness wasn't easy. There were many layers of resistance. I believed that to forgive him would mean dishonoring my mother and, even worse, approving of his behavior.

Once uncovered, it was easy to see that this belief was foolish. First of all, to forgive him would not dishonor my mother but only erase the impact and importance his wrong-doing had on my life. Second, to forgive him for his behavior would not mean endorsing it, but understanding the motives in order to disengage and become an objective judge of them. Furthermore, I realized that this belief–that I had to resent my father in order to honor my mother–gave me permission to harbor hostility against my father. I felt that the grudge I held against my father would bring him pain, causing him to suffer in return, and thus, would somehow make us even. What a distorted and nonsensical way of thinking. Until then, I hadn't seen myself as a vengeful person. It was not a pretty picture, and it was one more reason to let go of my resentment and let in forgiveness.

Resentment is about keeping internal account of personal damage unfairly inflicted by someone. Forgiveness is about erasing the account kept by resentment. Forgiveness is also about making the unfavorable impact of someone's wrongdoing less significant.

To proceed with forgiveness, I first had to assess the "damage." In order to determine what I had been deprived of by his absence, I had to imagine having an ideal father. I imagined the type of the person I wanted and needed him to be, the things we would have done together, the support and encouragement he would have given me, and the memories we would have built together. I wondered what would be different in my life today if I had had an ideal father. The answer was that I would feel more confident, less insecure. Then I asked myself what I would be more confident to do.

To my surprise, there was nothing specific, just this desire to have a higher overall sense of confidence. For the first time, I paid attention to what it meant to be confident. There were moments in my life when my confidence was strong and others when it was frail. Confidence seemed like a pool of energy within me, and I could generate the feeling from this pool according to the circumstances I found myself in. The level of my confidence fluctuated not because of my father's attitude, but because of my own convictions.

I continued to search for the things that he had irreparably damaged in me—the wrong deeds worthy of my resentment. Another feeling seemingly caused by my father's behavior was mistrust of men. His departure made me doubt other people's commitments. Trust is a choice we make to believe that another party holds some of our important values and standards.

As a grown person, I have the capacity to understand and express my values as well as to understand those of others. My father broke his unspoken promise to take care of me, and that behavior speaks only of his values, not mine. In addition, to see his values and attitudes as representative of the entire male population was childish. My choice to trust someone should have been based on the evaluation of common values applied to a specific situation, and not on my father's past behavior.

Further examining the damage, a feeling of unworthiness surfaced. To face this feeling, I had to challenge my point of view as the reason for my father's departure. By assuming that he didn't want me, I doubted *my* qualities. Ironically, never before did I examine *his* qualities. What if his abandonment had nothing to do with my worthiness? What if he was scared and insecure in his own capacity to be a good father? No one who feels confident and happy would abandon his family, especially during difficult times. A man cannot be proud of himself knowing he had left an ailing wife or abandoned his children. So, there must have been something more painful that drove him away. I couldn't comprehend what was so painful about being our father, what prompted him to make such a drastic decision, but I didn't need to. I was no longer the unwanted one.

Sometimes people choose between pleasure and pain; sometimes they must choose between two painful options. I choose to believe that my father left because he couldn't handle the demands of a large family. When faced with the choice between being a failure or being a coward, my father chose the latter. I don't think he intended to hurt me or damage my life. I have come to conclude that he had more faith in my strength to survive without him than he had in being a good father. After viewing him in this light, I realized that there was nothing to forgive him for. Nothing is permanently damaged as long as I can decide for myself. I don't know if my father is still alive, but it does not matter. He gave me my life and the freedom of choice that came with it. I realize that I am in charge, and I am free.

Chapter Twenty
About My Brother

✦

(Approval)

After my father left us when I was ten, my brother, who is fifteen-year older than I am, became the man of the house. Although he was never the authority figure that my mother was, unconsciously he became my father figure. My brother left Belgrade when I was sixteen and moved to Canada. I never realized the influence he had on my life until my late twenties, when I moved to Canada and met up with him again.

My brother is an inventor—a mechanic who redesigns machines. We are both very passionate about learning and discovering, especially about how things work. He's fascinated with machines, and I'm equally intrigued by the human machine. Whenever we met, we would spend hours talking about different gadgets or medical discoveries but never about our relationship.

It seemed that no one except for my brother could understand me very well. He understood my fascination with the mystery of things, and sharing ideas with him made me feel alive, complete, and at home. Still, something was missing. Every time my brother and I parted, I would have unsettling feelings. Although I felt close to him, there was a part of me that felt lonely, sad, and misunderstood. I was an adult with my own opinions, attitudes, and accomplishments, but somewhere deep inside, I was still a little girl looking up to my brother, waiting for his acceptance and approval.

Unfortunately, this need was not obvious from the beginning. For a very long time, I felt unsatisfied, somehow disappointed, but I could not understand why.

I looked forward to our conversations but dreaded my feelings upon our departure. With every visit there was hope that something would happen and that my feelings would change. The only thing that changed was the emergence of feelings of frustration. Not only did I feel unsatisfied, I was also frustrated and annoyed by my feelings. I could neither understand nor enjoy them.

One evening after leaving my brother's house, I wondered about my feelings. What was causing my emotional discomfort? What were the emotions I felt? After arriving home, I sat down and listed my feelings: sad, lonely, not understood, not recognized, little, scared, unsatisfied. The list was long and discombobulated. Then I looked for one feeling that could encompass all of the other feelings I was experiencing.

At first it seemed that my need for acceptance caused these feelings. Acceptance meant recognition of my values. Looking at my brother's behavior, I realized that he did recognize my values, not by praising them but by never disapproving of them. That was the old Serbian way of demonstrating love and acceptance nonverbally, and I was okay with it. Analyzing my situation helped me feel better, and I discovered another feeling more important than acceptance: approval. The missing piece was having my brother's approval!

Because I didn't know what I was seeking his approval *for*, I started from the other side; I asked myself what would happen if I got his approval. What would I do then? What would that feel like, and in what way would his approval impact my life? What made his approval so important? For an instant, I imagined that I got what I "needed" and wondered what would happen afterward. To my great surprise, I didn't have any answers. I was stunned. All my focus and energy were placed on something I that I had no idea how to use. I desperately needed something without knowing what do to when I got it.

Determined to solve my emotional confusion, I kept imagining what would happen if I did receive the approval I craved. As with my father, the answer was that I would feel more confident. Then what? What would more confidence allow me to do? I would be at peace with the decision I'd made to change my career. This realization pointed me toward looking deeper into everything that related to my profession.

Little by little, I recalled conversations during which I tried to discuss my interest in holistic healing approaches, conversations where my brother had either ignored my comments or verbalized his mistrust in alternative medicine. Those were the moments when I was feeling dismissed—not understood, frustrated, and consequently insecure about my decision and in need of his approval. My brother's dismissive attitude bruised my confidence and provoked me to doubt my decisions, as well as my qualities and capacities. Although it may sound ridiculous, I felt uncared for and unappreciated by my brother.

To better understand my feelings, I mentally returned to examine the word *approve* and questioned in what aspect of myself or my life had I been seeking my brother's support. To approve means to confirm or authorize the value—but what value? Was it that I am an intelligent, kind, or caring person? He already knew and recognized those qualities in me. Also, I didn't feel the need for those qualities to be confirmed. So I continued to wonder what else I was unconsciously trying to have "authorized" by my brother.

At that time of my life, I was studying homeopathy, a form of alternative medicine. Strongly attracted to this newly discovered medical approach, I felt myself drifting away from the security of the known and socially accepted conventional medicine. Venturing into something that was marginal by societal standards was scary, causing me to feel insecure and lonely, but also visionary and daring. I was desperately looking for the permission to be the person I was becoming. My new path was eliciting feelings of fear, uncertainty, and possibly even rejection by society. For that reason I needed someone important to me, like my brother, to agree with me and give me his blessing.

Mistakenly, in my need for approval, I was mixing and confusing different values. Looking for approval of a specific choice, I foolishly interpreted my brother's dismissive attitude toward alternative medicine as his unconcern for me. I internalized his lack of approval for my decision regarding homeopathy as disapproval of my entire personality.

If I had considered my specific need for him to approve my choice of alternative medicine, then I would have realized that my brother is not an expert in the health care field. I would have known not to look to him for answers that would alleviate my concerns. Being clear about my need for support, I could have stated my fears or concerns openly and communicated my need for his support clearly, and he could have given it to me. My brother could have approved of my wisdom to make a good choice or my courage to venture outside of conventional medicine.

The significance of this experience is that it helped me realize that regardless of whether my brother or anyone else approved of my choice, it was up to me to decide to trust my decision and build my confidence. Understanding my need for encouragement in order to build confidence was sufficient to create the feeling I needed. It was my path, and I had to believe in it. I was becoming a person who took the road less traveled. My emotions changed from insecurity, restlessness, and frustration to confidence and inner peace. Once again, I imagined getting my brother's approval. This time, I no longer needed it because I was approving of myself.

Chapter Twenty-One
Who Would Like Me?

✦

(Fear of Rejection)

In college, I had a roommate with whom I spent countless hours sharing ideas and experiences. Although I liked math and she liked poetry, I liked change and she liked routine, we had many things in common. But one thing separated us: in the mornings, I would make my bed, and she would leave hers unmade. For some unknown reason, her unmade bed bothered me. I am an orderly person and I felt irritated with my roommate's sloppiness. My inclination was to solve the problem, so I approached my roommate with honesty, sharing my concerns about the appearance of our apartment, my need to keep our rooms tidy, and asked for her cooperation.

My roommate made an occasional effort, but the overall situation didn't change. Her attitude fired up additional feelings in me. At first, I felt hurt that she didn't care about something that I clearly expressed as being important to me, and I became angry and judgmental, labeling her as inconsiderate. Powerless to change her attitude, I opted to ignore the situation, hoping for my emotions to subside.

The opposite effect happened. Time passed, and every time I saw the unmade bed, my feelings would surface with higher intensity until I couldn't ignore them any longer. No matter how much effort I put into rationalizing the situation—making it seem insignificant—my feelings were informing me differently. No matter how petty our disagreement, I was way too emotionally involved in it. The issue was pushing my emotional buttons, and I was clueless about how to stop it from happening. In addition, I felt frustrated with my own feelings because I could neither understand nor dismiss them.

I had to do something about the situation. After all, I was the only person reacting emotionally; my roommate seemed indifferent to it. Then I started wondering, how is it possible that one person has no emotional reaction to something while another feels so strongly about it? To solve *my* problem, I came up with a plan to go through a period of "personal training" to leave my bed undone and face my feelings.

As my training went on for a month, interesting things happened. Seeing my unmade bed triggered somewhat different emotions than seeing my roommate's unmade bed. Looking at her bed, I felt angry and irritated, but looking at mine provoked embarrassment and anxiety.

The anger and irritation felt against my roommate was clear; I was angry because my roommate violated the value of our friendship. As friends, we were to help each other, especially if one of us asked for a favor. Ironically, the way I viewed our commitments was distorted. I thought my request to make up her bed wasn't demanding a big effort from her, making it sound like no big deal, yet her lack of cooperation was making me upset. The irritation was like having a small rock in my shoe, a constant reminder of something being out of place.

Let's compare irritation to the feeling of being overwhelmed. With irritation, we give one little thing too much importance; when overwhelmed, we give too many things importance simultaneously. Going back to the emotions I felt when *my* bed was left unmade, I tried to understand the source of my embarrassment. I felt naked, exposed, wanting to cover up my "weakness." What about myself did I feel needed protection? The unmade bed meant "room in shambles," and "room in shambles" reflected negatively on my personality, suggesting laziness. My mother used to say, "Nobody wants a lazy person." If nobody wants a lazy person, then if I were perceived as lazy, I would be doomed to rejection and loneliness. With the fear of rejection exposed, the emotional beast of anxiety was released. Once surfaced, the extent of my anxiety was overwhelming. With such meaning attached to the appearance of my bed, it was no wonder I felt strongly about making the bed every morning! It is no surprise that I took my roommate's nonchalance personally. Making up the bed assured my worthiness for love and acceptance by others. Although it made no sense at the time, I came to realize that I had acquired this belief as a child.

I grew up in a single-parent family with four other siblings. To keep order in the house, my mother trained us—and I mean *trained* us—to make our beds as soon as we got up. Along with her discipline, she also instilled in us the belief that an unmade bed led to rejection—and tidiness to acceptance. Consequently, making my bed became automatic for me; it meant cultivating my virtues, having my mother's love, and gaining the acceptance of society. If my bed looked good, people would like me. It was that simple.

This realization was not enough, however, to quell my irritation; in fact, for awhile, it heightened it. Annoyed by the situation and especially with my emotional discomfort, I became angry with my mother. Her unreasonable rule was causing me trouble and anxiety. How dare she teach me something that would inflict emotional pain? The anger uncovered another nonsensical belief. My mother didn't do anything intentionally to hurt me. She just taught me the rules that worked for her. It was my responsibility to "update" my beliefs to match my standards and preferences.

My mother's rules and beliefs were no longer valid; I was free to choose my own reason for making–or not making-the bed. The situation was resolved by my becoming indifferent toward the state of my roommate's bed; after all, it did not reflect on my personal qualities. Regarding my own bed, most often I made it because I liked my room to look neat. But because an unmade bed no longer had the power to deprive me of love and acceptance, I was able to relax about it.

Although my feelings regarding the state of the bed faded away, my anxiety about rejection remained very much alive. Anxiety is like a reconnaissance scout telling us that we are about to face some situation with a *possible* danger. Anxiety alerted me to the fact that I could possibly miss the opportunity of being selected in some situation. The intent of anxiety is to alert you, to have you pay attention to the upcoming situation, so you can prepare better for the "encounter." It does not mean you are going to lose the battle, but that you need to evaluate your strengths and strategies. I feared rejection and wanted so badly to be liked and accepted. And I know that I am not alone. But what makes us so preoccupied with acceptance and rejection?

The unconscious and innate *need* for acceptance is linked to our survival. It all stems from our early childhood. If no one was willing to take care of us, our physical bodies would not continue to survive. In early childhood, our consciousness is not developed, and our need for acceptance is indiscriminately placed upon anybody. As our consciousness develops, we seek acceptance from certain people for selected things in order to assure our psychological survival. At this level, we may not consciously select our peers and colleagues for their acceptance of us, but we emotionally react when they don't.

As we develop and become aware of our likes and dislikes, skills and affinities, we seek people with whom we have a mental, emotional, and spiritual connection. The acceptance experienced from these selected people validates and helps keep our uniqueness alive. We learn innately that rejection is fatal. If an infant is rejected by society and left alone, it will not survive. If a child is rejected by society and left to develop on his own, he would atrophy mentally and emotionally.

Consequently, to stay alive we need the acceptance of others. Acceptance is nothing more but synchronizing energies between people. Imagine what it feels like when you are on the same "wave length" with another person; you feel accepted, grounded, and powerful. You feel more alive. Once we understand our need for acceptance, it becomes our responsibility to clarify our specific needs and make sure they are met appropriately.

The challenge we have with acceptance and rejection stems from our perception. Our awareness of our individual needs and who can provide for them is obscure and often unclear. In our perception of rejection we often regress to the basic, life-or-death need for acceptance that we felt as small children: we internalize rejection as terminal. For example, when suffering from a broken heart, we may feel lonely and unwanted by the entire world because one person rejected us. With our awareness focused on one specific person, we become oblivious to the love and acceptance we have from a number of people, including friends, coworkers, and/or relatives. We experience rejection as fatal and consequently give the feeling undeserved significance.

In order to lighten the detrimental feeling of rejection, let's look at it from an impersonal perspective. Imagine you are deciding to buy a pair of shoes. You consider the type of events for which you may need them, their comfort, style, and color, and then match their perceived qualities with your requirements. You do not accept or reject a particular pair of shoes, per se, but select those that best fit your criteria.

When you are in a situation of needing acceptance or fearing rejection, you need to ask yourself the following questions: For what specific personal value or standard am I seeking acceptance? What is the importance of these criteria? What would happen if the criteria do not get recognized and matched? What is the worst thing that can happen to me if the criteria are rejected? If my criteria for acceptance were met, what would be different in my life? Who else could fulfill my need for acceptance?

In my situation, tidiness made me feel comfortable, clean, clear, and efficient. With tidiness came order and I feel more alive when things are in order. Being neat was no longer the criterion for the acceptance of others, but for my own internal comfort. I loved myself and my life more when things around me were in order. With regard to my roommate, we agreed to keep common areas as neat as possible. To meet the rest of my requirements for order and a specific appearance of the apartment, I relied upon myself to take care of my needs. Regarding my self-worth and fear of rejection, I take each situation individually, thinking and feeling it as a process of deciding, and, to the extent that I am able, keeping an objective point of view.

If you think that this example seems trivial for the magnitude of my feelings, I would agree with you. But isn't that what usually happens when we emotionally overreact? My coaching experience with people having "panic" or "anxiety" attacks confirms that fear of rejection is often at the root of their problem. Generated by our instinct to survive and buried under other concerns, it sneaks up and "attacks." The significance of my story lies in the opportunity emotions provide us to look deeper into our beliefs and examine them.

Chapter Twenty-Two
Practicing Medicine

❖

(Self-Acceptance)

My mother wanted me to be a doctor. I never questioned her wish. Since I was an eager student and always willing to help people, medicine seemed a natural choice. Although my mother was no longer alive when I became a physician, I felt successful and proud of myself. I had accomplished my goal and fulfilled my mother's wish.

A year after finishing medical school, civil war broke out in my country, the former Yugoslavia. Dissatisfied with rising nationalism, I left Belgrade and moved to Montreal. A suitcase in each hand and hopes for living a better life, I was determined and fearless. With a medical degree in my pocket and a heart full of enthusiasm for healing the sick, I felt confident. But shortly after I moved to Canada, my hopes were shattered. I learned that Canadians had too many of their own medical graduates, and as a foreigner, my chances to practice medicine were minimal. There was a long waiting list for a fellowship, and I couldn't afford to wait. Disappointed and discouraged, I found myself in an emotional dilemma.

Standing at the crossroads of my career there were two paths: go back to my war-torn country and be a physician, or stay in Canada but give up practicing medicine. One road lead to caring for the sick in the midst of incomprehensible hatred, while the other road led to an unfamiliar territory paved with opportunities. Both choices were appealing and scary at the same time.

Returning to Belgrade was tempting because it would take me back to my family and friends. I wouldn't have to learn a new language, adapt to a different culture, or make my place in society. But returning to Belgrade included being in a place where the government demanded that you take sides and hate your neighbor, which was against my core values. I felt reluctant to even think about this option.

The option of staying in Canada was filled with possibilities to realize my dreams. This path wasn't burdened by war, but with uncertainty. I wasn't only scared about the unknown; I was also overwhelmed and tired. All the years spent in medical school looking forward to the day I could relax flashed in the front of my eyes. All that hard work and enthusiasm in vain!

I felt like a failure. Both options were clouded with disappointment. Returning to Belgrade meant announcing my defeat while staying in Canada meant renouncing my dream. I went back and forth between my choices until the heaviness of war outweighed the effort of starting life all over. Needless to say, I decided to stay in Canada.

What followed was my discovery of alternative medicine. Pursuing my desire to help others, I studied homeopathy, Chinese medicine, and neurolinguistic programming (NLP), and developed a passion for complementary healing approaches. But no matter how well I mastered my new venture, it never felt like a success.

Although passionate about having alternative views on—and approaches to—human well-being, I couldn't get rid of the feeling that I had somehow failed. I felt as if I had somehow betrayed conventional medicine, which was my first passion (and my mother's dream for me). Regardless of how much I rationalized that staying in Montreal was the wise choice, and no matter how much I enjoyed alternative approaches, deep inside I knew that I had given up on practicing medicine. I felt disgraced and somehow ashamed of myself. I saw a weakness in myself that I didn't like. Despite enjoying my new vocation, I also viewed it as being of lesser value.

Perceiving my choice as second-rate, I saw myself as being of a lesser value, too. After all, people appreciated doctors and considered alternative medicine practitioners as "voodoo" healers. I considered myself a reject. My self-esteem damaged, I often found myself excusing and justifying my choice, trying to prove to the entire society that I was valuable even though not functioning as a physician. No longer confident, but insecure and filled with self-doubt, I turned into a hesitant, apprehensive, and self-conscious person, feeling "not good enough." I felt that on the ride called "a happy life" I was not tall enough, smart enough, witty enough, or whatever else enough to reach the bar and be granted admission on the ride. In my eyes, everyone else made it except me.

Needless to say, I didn't enjoy the way I felt. I decided to explore what it really meant to fail. In my experience, to fail meant to not pass an exam. But who was the examiner and what was I being tested on? The old cliché "failing myself" didn't help. Looking for help in the *American Heritage* dictionary, I found that to fail is "to prove deficient; to perform ineffectively or inadequately; to decline as in strength or effectiveness; to disappoint or prove undependable to; to neglect or omit to perform."

Reading these definitions made me realize that the word *disappoint* resonated strongly within me. It evoked the image of my mother. And there she was—my most important examiner. I assumed that my not being a practicing physician would be disappointing to my mother, thereby failing her expectations. My mother was no longer alive, so I could not verify or clarify her expectations. I had to speculate on them. I wondered what her requirements were for passing in the category labeled success.

From her perspective, success probably meant an easier and more comfortable life than her own. Born in 1919, she grew up in an era in which women had no rights. At the age of sixteen, her parents gave her to a prominent man, wishing her a good life, not knowing that the groom had epilepsy. During one of his seizures, my mother got scared and ran home. No longer desirable for marriage and getting older, my mother waited a long time until she had the opportunity to remarry and fulfill her life's purpose of having children.

Not in a position to choose a partner or to get an education, my mother probably suffered emotionally. Like any parent, my mother desired a better life for me and for her other children. I do not know what prompted her to suggest a career in medicine—maybe because it represented a successful life, or maybe she saw my passion for helping others even then. Regardless of her motivation, I decided to view practicing conventional medicine as something separate from my success.

I still needed to see myself as successful through her eyes. I had to find criteria that transcended generations and social limitations. Guessing about my mother's criteria, I made a list of qualities that I knew she valued, and then I checked them off one by one:

- **Responsible.** Check. I have proven it by finishing school as planned and taking care of myself, my sisters, and the property our mother left us.

- **Dependable.** Check. My sisters, friends, and coworkers can count on me, taking my word at face value.

- **Respectful.** Check. I learned the values my mother taught me, and I appreciated other people's time, effort, and affection.

- **Respected.** Check. Many people confirm this to me through their love and friendship.

- **Self-reliant.** Check. I made my own living and had earned my own place in society.

- **Diligent**. Check. I study hard and work hard.

Looking at the checked-off list, I felt satisfied and accomplished. I was proud of myself, and knew that my mother would be proud, too.

After the euphoria of being freed from the feeling of failure subsided, I was left with the aftertaste of another feeling. All previously checked feelings were common, and my unusual passion for alternative medicine and other alternative views were unaccounted for. Because of my unconventional interests, I felt weird and doubtful of my qualities. I shifted into a mode of self-criticism, and my high-energy enthusiasm was rapidly spiraling downward. Sadness, discouragement, and low self-esteem were only a few of the feelings that surfaced.

Have you ever noticed how when you start feeling demoralized your feelings turn into a party of "loser" emotions? Dwelling on my quirkiness and questioning who would like me, I started deepening my self-rejection, inflicting emotional pain and suffering upon myself, ironically under the guise of self-preparation and self-protection. I started comparing myself to others, looking for attributes or things that I did *not* have, feeling vulnerable, shaky, unsupported, and scoring ever low on my self-esteem test.

I don't know what makes us do this, but the moment we doubt the value of our uniqueness, we become cruel self-examiners. We scrutinize ourselves, searching for deficiencies and defects in our character until we become "not good enough."

Aware of the situation, I closed the floodgate of draining emotions and examined this business of cruel self-evaluation. Instead of having rejection as my focal point, my decision was to conduct an assessment of my values and characteristics with self-acceptance as my intent. I was on a mission of making peace with my uniqueness, willing and ready to dig deep inside. I realized that most of my self-inflicted emotional pain came from a lack of clarity.

For example, the concept of not being good enough was extremely vague. Enough means just the right amount. The usual implication of feeling "not good enough" is that we are not good enough for someone to love us. But have we ever determined how much love is enough for us? How do we know that amount? And if enough is the "right amount," then enough love is the right amount for what? Is it to survive? Or is it to have confidence? And, if so, enough confidence to do what?

Concentrating on self-acceptance, I examined myself through the eyes of a good friend. I identified the characteristics and affinities which, if displayed by a friend, I would embrace and admire. Next, I recognized those that I myself didn't enjoy and examined them even further.

Although I decided to change my undesirable traits, I was concerned that they could still be a potential cause for my feelings of rejection and failure. So, I thought of my real friends and examined their characteristics more specifically, wondering what would make me not want to have them as friends. I realized that not only was I content with them, but I rather enjoyed their individualities. Seeing in this new light, I felt happy with my odd self. I embraced the unusual interests that had previously led to my self-rejection. Choosing to be comfortable in my own skin, my uncommon interests and unusual path were automatically transformed to my advantage and evoked a sense of fulfillment.

Self-acceptance is the integration of personal awareness and values. First, we become aware of our unique skills and affinities, then we make them part of our value system. Self-acceptance comes as a result of the process of self-evaluation. The intersection of self-evaluation and self-acceptance is called self-esteem.

Self-esteem is like a report card. As emotions are messengers informing us about a specific situation needing our attention, a feeling of "low self-esteem" is also a messenger. Whenever we score low on our personal evaluation, we are asked to re-examine the accuracy and validity of the accounted criteria.

Over the years, my self-esteem increased because I had many opportunities to change or accept my unique self. Life brings me face to face with various situations, and the feelings of failing, insecurity, or self-rejection come and go. Meanwhile, I have grown more agile in dealing with and transforming them.

Regardless of whether you grew up in a functional or dysfunctional family, there will be a point in your life when you will be working on self-acceptance. We are unique, and thus we inevitably question our identity and seek approval and acceptance from our parents or siblings. Reading my story, you may find that you are not alone in dealing with this sensitive issue. Hopefully, you have found a helpful guideline to support you in this aim.

Chapter Twenty-Three
My Mother's Death

✦

(Guilt)

My mother was still asleep. Since January, illness had taken a bad turn. She was spending increasingly more time in bed, sleeping a lot. Although her authority and presence never changed, it was unusual seeing her quiet and immobile. Since she couldn't attend to her own needs any longer, my siblings and I shared time by her side. Being the youngest, and with the least important chores, I was assigned the most time by my mother's bedside.

It was midmorning on Sunday, March 25, 1979. There was nothing to do. I recalled my previous evening "shift." It had been kind of fun. Sitting in the quiet room with dimmed lights and nothing to do was great for a dreamer like me. The evening shifts seemed easier than the day shifts. During the day, my friends were available to play, and the temptations for a fourteen-year-old were endless. Sitting still on a sunny Sunday was challenging.

My mother opened her eyes and asked me for pain medicine. I asked if she needed anything else, she shook her head no and drifted back to sleep. I sat there quietly for some time.

Everyone else was doing something active: my brother was cleaning the garage, one sister was at the market grocery shopping, and the other sister was cooking. Becoming even more bored and restless, imagining all the things I could be doing, I decided to cheat on my duty. My decision was firm that I would not neglect my duty, just modify it a little. My plan was to go to the other part of the house and watch my favorite TV show for only short periods of time, but keep checking on my mother.

I don't recall if it was because I stayed for too long or if it was just a matter of timing, but on my third run back to see my mom, I found her gasping for air. I tried to ask her questions; she didn't respond. I yelled for my brother and sister.

They both ran into the room. Pushing me aside, they tried to resuscitate her. Finally they stopped, looked at each other, and then turned around and started crying. My mother had just died.

The following days were filled with commotion—making funeral arrangements, having family and friends visiting, going to school and announcing the bad news, organizing everything, and acquiring new duties. I felt confused but mostly scared. All the time I'd spent by my mother's bedside, I never thought about death. Nobody ever talked about it, and we had never had anyone die before. Not knowing death's consequences, I was concerned. But most of all, I felt nervous and afraid that I had made a mistake and would be punished for it. We were usually punished if we had poor report cards, broke a glass, or neglected a duty. I believed that by leaving my mother's room, I had contributed to her death. What if I had missed the opportunity to save her? I was petrified imagining what could happen to me if anyone knew about my misbehavior.

At first, I kept my misstep a secret. I played the events of that morning over and over in my head, re-evaluating my choices and decisions and deeply regretting my decision to watch TV. Afraid to bring up the subject and be discovered, I avoided talking about how much I missed my mom. I wished that I could turn back time. Filled with sadness, guilt, shame, and fear, I kept my secret to myself.

Life went on. We were settled in our daily routine when I realized that there were no beatings any longer and that I was not reprimanded for my mistakes. Weighted with guilt but no longer fearing beatings, I confessed to my older sister. We talked a long time about what happened, and she assured me that there was no wrong done. I accepted her "verdict" with relief, but unbeknownst to me, I kept the memory and judgment of my decision in the back of my mind.

It wouldn't be until many years later while remembering my childhood experiences that my feelings of guilt resurfaced. I blamed myself for not keeping my promise to take care of my mother when I *knew* she depended on me. Although I had mentally accepted that there was nothing in my power to save my mother, I was nevertheless hurting emotionally. The meaning given to my decision to leave the room and watch TV was causing me pain. When my mother died, I concluded that something was wrong with me. Somehow I came to the conclusion that my willpower was defective because it was its weakness that led me to make a poor choice. No matter how much effort I put into strengthening my will or keeping my word, deep inside I felt like a liar. I didn't like myself because of my flaw, and I assumed that others who loved me only felt that way because they didn't know the "truth." My convoluted way of thinking was calling for immediate intervention.

Understanding my feelings of regret was easier than dealing with the guilt. I deeply regretted my decision to leave my mother's bedside. If I could go back in time, I would have chosen differently. It seemed that I had learned from it and that I was able to let go of regret, but overcoming guilt was more difficult. The *American Heritage* dictionary refers to guilt as "a feeling of being responsible for an offense or crime or self-reproach for supposed inadequacy or wrongdoing." I looked at myself as the fourteen-year-old girl I was then and tried to understand her decision from my adult point of view. The little girl was a child who wanted to play. Yes, the fourteen-year-old girl made a mistake, but she didn't commit a crime. As a child, I was incapable of foreseeing the larger consequences of my decisions. It wasn't my absence that caused my mother's death. Maybe my presence could have made it easier for her. Maybe if I had held her hand or stroked her hair, she could have passed more peacefully. As a child, I couldn't have known what to do to help her transition worlds. I realize now that it wasn't my willpower that was inadequate but my awareness. Furthermore, the fact that I played out a possibility of rectifying the damage helped me feel less guilty and more neutral about the situation. I forgave the little girl for the wrongdoing, and she helped me realize that what my mother needed was not in my power to give her at the time. Guilt had no purpose.

Guilt is a feeling tied to our moral values, and every person experiences it. The significance of the story told is in seeing how I found my way out of guilt, while preserving the integrity of my personal values. The purpose of guilt is to teach us to make better decisions; once we learn how, we have to know to move on.

The Game of Life

It is not because things are difficult that we do not dare; it is because we do not dare that they are difficult.

Seneca the Elder

Most people believe that life is about the pursuit of happiness. Unfortunately, they are unaware that if the objective of life were to have only one feeling, human life would be one long, boring experience. Instead of searching for just happiness, we should strive to attain an inner state of personal strength and balance while feeling a full spectrum—a rainbow—of experiences.

People are afraid of their feelings because they do not understand them. Contrary to general belief, emotions are neither elusive or intangible, nor useless intruders to our lives. They are important personal messengers with distinctive roles and benevolent intents. Emotions are our personal servants assisting us in experiencing and expressing our power and uniqueness; they help us make decisions and define our lives.

Imagine the journey of man as a video game called the *Game of Life.* Each human is especially "designed" for this game and thus given a unique role, internally encoded. To confirm our authenticity, each individual has a personal genetic make-up—a combination of likes and dislikes, strengths and weaknesses, skills and shortcomings. To demonstrate that we are not interchangeable with other players, each of us faces a unique set of personal life circumstances. We play this game as we go through life by searching for the circumstances that will stimulate the unfolding of our uniqueness. We recognize those circumstances when we emotionally react to them. To play this game we are given free will and the capacity to make decisions.

Thinking and feeling help us make decisions, therefore progressing in the game. Feeling provides a sense of direction, and thinking helps adjust the course. Feelings help us navigate the path of our unique lives; "positive" feelings tell us we are in the flow, and "negative" feelings inform us about the need to adjust our course.

The main objectives of the game are to keep our awareness and knowledge expanding and our feelings engaged. The challenge to meeting our objective is to stay open-minded and open-hearted. If one of the two closes, our progress halts.

In any video game, there are levels of skills for players to transcend. In the *Game of Life*, we progress and reach new personal levels defined by "altitude" and "aptitude." We reach new levels of personal altitude when we climb the inner spiral staircase of consciousness; the more we are aware of our uniqueness and the way it relates to society, the higher we stand. We gain new levels of personal aptitude by experiencing inner flexibility and strength; the better we are at understanding our thoughts, feelings, and decisions, the more empowered we feel, and the more enjoyment we find in life.

Because this is not an ordinary game, our progress happens in three dimensions simultaneously: We are discovering, expressing, and expanding our unique personalities all at the same time. The game is similar to watching our life unfold on three screens where colors and sharpness of the image depend on the clarity of our thoughts and feelings. In an intense argument, you can learn what ticks you off, how you relate to the other person, and test different attitudes.

This game is like no other game; the destination and the speed do not matter. Players don't start or finish at the same time. There are always some players joining and some players leaving the game. The past and the future serve as references only; the action is in the present. It is important to mention that the experiences we accumulate along the path are nothing but the benchmarks for our transformation.

Because the objective of the game is to stay connected to the flow of life, we have to keep internally expanding. To promote inner growth, we meet various obstacles along our path. Feelings of boredom and vitality serve as the inner gauge of personal involvement in life. When the game of life is challenging, making our thinking and feeling stretch and expand, we feel immersed and alive. The more absorbed we are, the more we enjoy the game. When the *Game of Life* fails to promote the use of our skills or it does not stimulate our uniqueness to unfold, the game appears too easy, and we become disengaged.

Have you ever wondered why it is that challenging games keep us engaged and riveted, while challenging life circumstances make us discouraged and overwhelmed? It is because we don't view life as a game, and we don't view our feelings as being our allies. We fight with our feelings, trying to ignore or control them, instead of understanding and considering their messages. Very often, our emotional turmoil is caused by limited or conflicting beliefs. Heeding the messages of our emotions can help us discover and transform those beliefs, guiding us to find unique ways to live the most fulfilling life.

Understanding and managing emotions can be challenging but with a playful attitude it can be a lot of fun. Emotions are friendly messengers helping you engage in life the way you choose.

I hope that the material provided in this book has encouraged you to open your mind and view your emotions in a different light. Remember, emotions are *your* servants. Make your mind a captive audience to your feelings, but in a new way; instead of letting your feelings intimidate you, befriend them and start using them to empower your decisions. Once in charge of your own emotional buttons, you become the master of your game.

Tables

Table 1

Sensation of Energy

This list offers guidelines for recognizing the internal sensations that describe your inner energy, helping you to distinguish between different feelings.

Feeling	Sensation of Energy
Admiration	Open. Energy flows out then in. You feel energized and a slight boost
Ambitious	Open. Energy flows out openly. You feel pulled forward, energized and limitless
Angry	Closed. Energy builds against something specific; sensation of being empowered and tense
Anticipation	Open. Energy increases and flows out; sensation of slight pull forward
Anxious	Closed. Energy is pulling in or closing in; restless sensation
Ashamed	Closed. Energy collapses; sensation of folding in or sinking
Confidence	Open. Energy exudes from your entire being. You feel centered, grounded, energized, and internally in harmony
Contentment	Open. The energy flow is subtle. Energy is slightly increasing because there is no internal tension. You feel a peaceful fullness
Courage	Open. Energy concentrated. You feel strong and firmly grounded
Deceived	Closed. Energy deflated and pulling in and away
Desperate	Closed. Energy flow is sinking inward, as if pulled down or back; sensation as if your hold is slipping
Determined	Open. The flow of energy is moving out, channeled like a laser beam from you to your objective. You feel like something is propelling you
Disappointed	Closed. Energy flows inward and stops; sensation of being dropped
Dishonest	Closed. Energy drawn toward the center of your being; sensation of something unsettled
Faith	Open. Energy flows to you from something greater than you are. You feel energized and supported
Fearful/afraid	Closed. Energy confined within; sensation of internal shrinking
Frustration	Closed. Energy flows out and stops, as if hitting an obstacle; sensation of being halted

Feeling	Sensation of Energy
Guilty	Closed. Energy drawn toward a specific spot; irritating sensation
Happy	Open. An excess of energy is releasing. You feel intensely energized
Hateful/vindictive	Closed. Energy surges out with the intensity and the impulse to do harm
Helpless	Closed. Energy drains. You feel weakened and alone
Honest	Open. Energy is steady and centered. You feel a strong internal core
Hope	Open. Energy is heightened and flows freely. You feel open to receive
Hopeless	Closed. Energy is enclosed. You feel trapped
Insecure	Closed. Sensation of energy constantly changing and decreasing
Integrity	Open. Energy flows vertically; sensation of an internal sync
Joy	Open. Energy exudes and lingers around
Lonely	Closed. Energy level low; sensation of being held down
Longing	Open. Energy is stretched; sensation of a slight pull forward and a strong tug back
Love	Open. Energy flows from you to another person, back and forth, making a figure eight. You feel connected and energized
Loyal	Open. Energy flows in and out in a linear fashion. You feel a bond
Needy	Closed. Energy flows in then drains out. You feel empty and clingy
Overwhelmed	Closed. Energy oppressed; sensation of tension and fragility
Passion	Open. Energy flows out as if pulled by something specific. You feel perpetually recharged
Patient	Open. The flow is within and toward a center; sensation of stability, holding firmly, rooted
Proud	Open. The energy exudes from within. You feel bigger and more stable
Rejected	Closed. Sensation of being confined and excluded. Energy shrinks
Responsible	Open. Energy internally anchored circulating toward and from the destined person or object
Satisfaction	Open. Energy flows in and fills the void. You feel relief
Sexy	Open. Energy has two directions: exuding out and pulling things in. You feel strongly energized and magnetic

Feeling	Sensation of Energy
Stressed	Closed. Energy is building up; sensation of tension on the verge of bursting
Successful	Open. Energy rises, as if boosted to a new level.
Suspicious	Closed. Energy goes back and forth; sensation of being protective and highly alert
Trust	Open. Energy extends out to something specific. You feel at the same time, both reaching out and being connected
Vain/arrogant	Open. Energy flows out and pushes down; sensation of height or being inflated
Worried	Closed. Energy is churning within; sensation of tension and weakness from being worn down

Table 2
Emotion Vocabulary

This list provides a variety of words to help you describe your feelings and differentiate your experiences. The purpose of this list is to assist you in becoming emotionally literate.

A	B	Clever	Desired
Accomplished	Beautiful	Combative	Desperate
Adequate	Betrayed	Comfortable	Destructive
Adamant	Bewildered	Competitive	Determined
Admiring	Bitter	Condemned	Devoted
Admired	Blissful	Condescending	Different
Affectionate	Bold	Confident	Dignity
Agitated	Bored	Conflicted	Diminished
Aggressive	Bothered	Confused	Discomfort
Agony	Brave	Conspicuous	Disgust
Alive	Burdened	Contented	Dishonest
Alone	C	Confident	Disenchanted
Ambivalent	Calm	Contrite	Disillusioned
Annoyed	Capable	Curiosity	Dissatisfied
Apathetic	Captivated	Cruel	Displeased
Appreciated	Caring	Crushed	Distracted
Arrogant	Challenged	Culpable	Disrespected
Astounded	Charmed	D	Distraught
Attraction	Cheated	Daring	Distant
Audacious	Cheerful	Deceitful	Destroy
Aware	Childish	Defeated	Disturbed
Awake	Clean	Defiant	Disturbing
Awed	Clear	Delighted	Dominated

Divided	Glad	Intimidated	Mystical
Doubtful	Grateful	Intrigued	**N**
E	Greedy	Isolated	Naughty
Eager	Grief	**J**	Neat
Economical	Groovy	Jealousy	Nervous
Elated	Guilty	Joyous	**O**
Empty	Gullible	**K**	Obnoxious
Energetic	**H**	Kind	Obsessed
Envious	Happy	Keen	Odd
Excited	Hate	**L**	Opposed
Exasperated	Helpful	Laconic	Outraged
Exhausted	Helpless	Lazy	Overwhelmed
F	Homesick	Left Out	**P**
Faith	Honest	Lonely	Pain
Faithful	Honored	Longing	Panicked
Fascinated	Hurt	Love	Paralyzed
Fearful	Hysterical	Loving	Peaceful
Forceful	**I**	Loved	Persecuted
Flustered	Ignored	Lust	Petrified
Foolish	Impatient	**M**	Picked At
Frantic	Impressed	Mad	Pity
Frustrated	Indecisive	Mean	Playful
Free	Infatuated	Melancholy	Pleased
Frightened	Infuriated	Mischievous	Powerful
Frugal	Injured	Miserable	Polite
Furious	Irritable	Mistaken	Polluted
G	Insecure	Misunderstood	Pressured
Giddy	Inspired	Modest	Protected

Proud	Shocked	Terrified	**Y**
Q	Shy	Threatened	Yearning
Quarrelsome	Secure	Tired	**Z**
Quiet	Serious	Timid	Zealous
R	Silly	Trapped	
Rage	Skeptical	Trusting	
Recognized	Sneaky	Trusted	
Refreshed	Spiteful	Trustworthy	
Regret	Startled	Troubled	
Rejected	Strange	**U**	
Relaxed	Strangled	Ugly	
Reluctant	Strong	Uneasy	
Relieved	Stuffed	Unpleasant	
Remorse	Stupid	Unsettled	
Resentful	Stunned	Useful	
Resisting	Submissive	Useless	
Restless	Subservient	**V**	
Restrained	Suffering	Violent	
Reserved	Sure	Vulnerable	
Respected	Suspicious	Vacillating	
Reverent	Sympathy	Victorious	
Rewarded	**T**	**W**	
Ridiculous	Talkative	Wicked	
Righteous	Taciturn	Weak	
S	Tempted	Weird	
Sad	Tenacious	Wonderful	
Satisfied	Tenuous	Weepy	
Scared	Tense	Worried	

Table 3
Emotion Messages

This table offers you an idea about the meanings and messages of emotions. It also gives you coaching suggestions to help you change your emotional experience or make different choices.

Feeling	Emotion Messages	Coaching Suggestions
Angry	An important value of yours has been violated, and you oppose the act of violation	Take note of the important value, and choose your attitude
Anticipation	There is a possibility of something happening, and you believe it will be pleasurable	Remember what it feels like, and use it instead of apprehension
Anxious	You perceive there is danger waiting for you in the future	Identify and evaluate the "danger," then prepare to overcome it
Apprehension	It is possible that something specific could happen, and you believe it will be troublesome	Remember it is a possibility, not a probability. Choose your belief, focus, and attitude
Arrogant	You feel empowered because you perceive your standards as more important than someone else's	It creates distance with others, make sure your intention is clear
Ashamed	You think you lost someone's favor, love, or respect because of your improper deed or attitude	Reevaluate the relevance and significance of your shameful deed
Being Perfect	You recognize specific values or standards as having reached their ideal place or ideal fit	"Ideal fit" refers to a specific moment/situation. Do not be rigid
Bored	You are not using your skills or expressing your uniqueness	Identify the skills you could use immediately
Criticized	Someone is describing unfavorable details for a specific situation	The key word is unfavorable. Find what is favorable and move on
Deceived	You realize that your perception, and thus your projected expectation, differs from your experience	Revise your expectation and whether your values or standards match the other person's

Feeling	Emotion Messages	Coaching Suggestions
Desperate	You perceive that there is an unmet need vital to your survival; you're running out of energy and hope	Did you explore every possibility? How much energy do you have left?
Disappointed	Your expectations and experiences differ; you lost hope with regard to meeting a specific expectation	You have two choices: move on or change your expectations to restore your hope
Doubtful	You are alerted to reevaluate and reconsider relevant criteria in order to make a congruent decision	It does not mean wrong decision but the opportunity to improve your position
Envious	You perceive that you have the right, but not the chance, to have something	Focus on your capacity, not your right, to get what you want
Fearful	You perceive something as possibly harmful and overpowering in relation to your capacity to handle it	Adjust your perception: reevaluate the danger and your capacity to overcome it
Frustrated	Your expectation is in your sight but out of your reach	Modify your approach or your expectation
Guilty	You made a choice that disturbed someone's well-being	Learn about the consequence of your decision. Adjust your intention and attitude
Helpless	You feel unable to complete an arduous task with nothing or no one to supplement your weakness	Reevaluate your strength, the difficulty of the task, and what would be appropriate help
Hopeless	You believe there is no possibility for something to happen	It is your choice to believe what is possible and in your capacity to generate hope
Indifferent	You are not acknowledging anything as significant	This attitude gives you, if positive, time to evaluate your feelings, and if negative, numbness
Insecure	You consider your attributes as insufficient to successfully handle a specific situation	Be precise. Identify, itemize, and re-assess your characteristics and skills that are relevant
Lonely	You believe there is no one willing to share experiences you desire	Expand your perception. Focus on one activity you desire. Be creative. Take action

Feeling	Emotion Messages	Coaching Suggestions
Longing	Something is holding you back and preventing you from fulfilling your desire	Reevaluate what is holding you back. Change your perception and beliefs
Perfectionist	You perceive that you can bring a specific value or standard to a new level	Avoid making rules. Focus on vision, and act as a leader
Regretful	A choice you made is either incongruent with your values or unpleasant to experience	You gained valuable information. Take mental note and move on
Rejected	Your characteristics or values are unfavorable in a specific situation	Recognize that specific characteristics are mismatched, not the entire you
Stressed (outside)	You are considering too many things as equally important	Prioritize your tasks
Stressed (inside)	The image of you (ego) and the authentic you are incongruent	Focus on what you "could be" not what you "should be"
Worry	You perceive that something or someone, including yourself, lacks strength or resources to resist a possible danger	Adjust your perception. You may be underestimating the resources or overestimating the danger

About the Author

Emina Karamanovski, M.D., is a pioneer in the field of using emotions to their fullest potential. Realizing the importance of emotions, she studied different methods that address positive thinking or emotion management, personally testing each of them. Influenced primarily by Viktor Frankl's logotherapy, Milton H. Erickson's hypnotherapy, and research in the domain of heart science, Dr. Karamanovski developed her own unique approach to strengthening emotional intelligence. Her approach is innovative: emotions are messengers, and by understanding their messages we can improve our emotional intelligence. Her teaching is empowering. Once we learn the language of emotions, we gain the ability to deliberately choose our feelings and thus decide how we want to emotionally engage in life.

A native of former Yugoslavia, now Serbia, she completed medical school at the University of Belgrade. In 1991, she moved to Canada and then later to the United States. Pursuing her interests, in 2000 she earned a Coaching Certification from HeartMath. She obtained a Diplomate in Logotherapy credential from the Viktor Frankl Institute of Logotherapy in 2001. She is licensed by Excellence Quest and Richard Bandler as a Practitioner of Neuro-Linguistic Programming. Dr. Karamanovski completed Certified Coach Intensive Program by CoachVille in 2003 and is currently in the process of obtaining her Professional Coach Certified license (PCC) from the International Coach Federation.

Believing that in emotional matters people are not ill but uneducated, and thus don't need healing but guidance toward better decision making, Dr. Karamanovski started coaching individuals on a one-on-one basis. Since starting her private practice as an emotion coach in 2000, she has been helping people transform their emotional dilemmas and traumas into emotional clarity and empowerment. In addition to individual coaching, Emina offers group training and seminars in Dallas, Texas, where she currently resides.

Bibliography

Benson, H. *Timeless Healing*. New York: Fireside (Simon & Schuster), 1997.

Buhner, S. H. *The Secret Teachings of Plants*. Rochester, Vermont: Bear & Company, 2004.

Childre, D., and B. Crayer. *From Chaos to Coherence*. Woburn, MA: Butterworth-Heinemann, 1999.

Childre, D., and H. Martin. *The HeartMath® Solutions*. San Francisco: HarperCollins Publishers Inc, 1999.

Damasio, A. *Descartes' Error*. New York: Avon Books, 1994.

Frankl, V.E. *Man's Search for Meaning*. New York: Washington Square Press, 1959.

Goleman, D. *Emotional Intelligence*. New York: A Bantam Book, 1994.

Gordon, D., and M. Meyers-Anderson. *Phoenix, Therapeutic Patterns of Milton H. Erickson*. Cupertino, CA: Meta Publications, 1981.

Keen, S. *Learning to Fly*. New York: Broadway Books, 1999.

LeDoux, J. *The Emotional Brain*. New York: A Touchstone Book by Simon & Schuster, 1996.

Lipton, B. *The Biology of Belief*. Santa Rosa, CA: Mountain of Love, 2005.

Contact Information

More information on Emina Karamanovski's work and her one-on-
one coaching, seminars, and workshops can be found at
www.emina.net
www.freedomcoaching.com

978-0-595-41731-5
0-595-41731-0

Printed in the United States
201493BV00001B/151-555/P